Pets Handbook

OTHER TITLES IN THIS SERIES

PETS HANDBOOK

By Arthur Butterfield

BANCROFT · London, W. 1

First published in 1969 by Bancroft Books.
© Copyright 1969 by B.P.C. Publishing Limited, London, W. 1
All rights reserved.
Printed in Germany.
SBN 430 00358 7

Contents

Introduction

One of the first questions a would-be pet-keeper should ask himself or herself is, Am I fit to have a pet? The query is not as frivolous as it sounds. The responsibility resting on you, after you have introduced a new pet into your home, is inescapable. After all, the animal did not ask you to buy it. It relies on you entirely for its comfort, health, happiness, and very existence. Unless you are prepared to spend money, time, and a great deal of patience on your pet, with a real affection for it, it might be that stamps or paperweights are more in your line.

Before you beg, buy, or borrow a pet, there are several factors to be considered. Can you afford, not only the initial cost, but the cost of housing and feeding the animal, maybe for years? Have you got room enough to house it? A tiny St. Bernard puppy is no trouble in a small flat—for the first few months... later, it would be rather like keeping a rabbit in a hamster's cage. Are there children in your family? Are you prepared to train *them* to look after animals, and live with them? What about other pets in the house, such as dogs and cats? Have you made allowances for any reaction there? What about holidays and travel? Who looks after your pets while you're away?

These questions highlight some of the perils of buying on impulse. So many people, especially children, feel sorry for a little bundle of fur in the corner of a pet shop window, plonk down their shillings and take it home with them. Then their troubles begin. Often they have no idea how to house or feed the creature. The result is that the owner soon gets tired of the pet and after a few days it is left to fend for itself—an abject heap of misery.

This book is intended to be a comprehensive guide to as wide a selection of pets as possible. It does not pretend to give specialist advice on ailments, the construction of hutches and cages, nor the breeding of exotic varieties. What it does give you is elementary common sense information on the selection, housing, feeding, grooming, training, and simple nursing of all the popular pets, together with some less familiar but attractive ones.

DOGS AND CATS

Dogs

Dogs have a very long history. They are all probably
descended from a primitive wolf-like animal that lived
about 10 million years ago. Wolves, jackals, foxes, coyotes.
and other wild dogs all came from this first parent. About
20,000 years ago Stone Age men trained dogs to hunt
game. The Ancient Egyptians developed a greyhound-like
dog to run down antelopes about 8,000 years ago.

The oldest pure breed of dog is probably the Saluki,
developed as a hunting dog by the Ancient Egyptians. The

Ancient Greeks developed the Mastiff as a guard and fighting dog. The Romans also used Mastiffs, and kept several breeds of dogs as pets.

Buying

Once you decide to have a dog as a pet, you are immediately faced with several problems. What sort of dog to buy? Should it be large, medium or small? Should it be a dog or a bitch? Is it better to have a pedigree animal, or a mongrel?

The size of animal you buy really depends on where you live. A large, sporting type of dog, such as an Irish Setter, a Bloodhound, or a Labrador, needs a roomy house in the country. In addition to large grounds or plenty of open country for exercise, these large dogs also need to be taken for walks and runs *daily*. This daily controlled exercise seems to be an essential ingredient for the happiness of most dogs. Another item to think about, when buying a big dog, is the daily food bill. These animals have appetites to match their size. One of the great advantages of a large dog is that it often has a more placid temperament than the smaller breeds, and of course a big dog makes a good guard by its very presence.

Medium-sized dogs such as terriers, Whippets, and Beagles are a compromise, and are well adapt to life either in the town or in the country. They are large enough to deter unwelcome visitors, and small enough to live in a flat, without breaking the grocery budget. They are deservedly popular.

The smallest breeds are the miniatures and "toys". These include Toy Poodles, Dachshunds, Pomeranians, and Chihuahuas. Their advantage lies in the small space they take up, and the comparatively little food they eat. On the other hand many of the overbred miniatures are highly strung animals, and their high-pitched barking often takes some getting used to. But even these tiny, very portable dogs need a certain amount of exercise each day if they are to remain healthy.

The question of sex is often the last to be considered by a prospective buyer. Some experts hold that bitches are more affectionate than dogs, but others claim that it depends on the individual animal. Bitches are generally less aggressive than dogs, and are also less inclined to wander off from their homes. Their great disadvantage is that twice a year they come in season. This period lasts for about 3 weeks each time. There are a number of proprietary tablets on the market that you can give the bitch; these will discourage visiting dogs.

Whether you buy a mongrel or a pedigree specimen will largely depend on your bank balance. Mongrels are often given away free to "good homes". Pedigree dogs obtained from a recognized breeder have all the advantages of a known history. The breeder is an expert, and will no doubt be able to find you just the dog you need. You are paying for his knowledge, so you might as well use it.

The trouble with mongrels is that you can never be sure how a puppy will turn out. Mongrels are not necessarily stronger or more intelligent than pedigree dogs. They may have some inbred hereditary disease that only shows itself in certain generations. Their parents may have suffered from malnutrition—a condition that is bound to show itself in some weakness of the offspring. However, when all is said and done, many owners of "ordinary" mongrel dogs would not exchange their pets for the finest pedigree specimens in the world. Mongrels are just as affectionate, and often just as attractive in appearance, as many high-priced pure-bred dogs.

When inspecting a litter of puppies, mongrel or pedigree, there are certain signs to look for. Pick out the strong, playful, inquisitive puppy. Don't take the runt of the litter, the little shy one that cowers away in a corner, however sorry you may feel for it. A good healthy puppy has bright eyes and loose skin round his body. Make sure that he has been wormed before you accept him. Many young puppies suffer from worms in their first few weeks, and there are a number of medicines on the market to cope with this common complaint.

What age should the dog be when you buy him? He should be completely weaned. This occurs between 8 and 12 weeks. But a puppy of that age will almost certainly not yet be house-trained. If you want to include that advantage, you would do better to buy a dog about 6 months old, even if you have to pay a little more.

Finally, where to buy. Breeders advertise in the dog papers (*Dog World, Our Dogs,* and others), and also in some of the dailies and weeklies. The Kennel Club will also help you. Non-pedigree dogs can be bought in pet shops for anything from a few shillings to a few guineas; local vets, animal clinics, and the R.S.P.C.A. also frequently have unwanted puppies for disposal. Your local paper will also advertise dogs for sale regularly.

Housing

Once you have bought your puppy, the question of where to put him arises. It should be said right away that unless your dog is a working animal—that is, a dog kept for hunting, rounding up sheep, or drawing sledges across icy wastes—it is best to let him sleep indoors. Outdoor kennels are fine for packs of Foxhounds, but a pet should be a *household* pet.

The two greatest enemies of a dog's health and comfort are damp and draughts. His bed should therefore be put in a draught-free place, and raised off the floor. A secluded corner of a roomy kitchen will often meet these requirements. Rectangular canvas beds are sold in some pet shops. These are excellent, as are some of the fibreglass versions, which are easily and quickly wiped down. Dogs baskets are a little less useful, especially for large dogs. The baskets are usually round and a dog likes to stretch to his full length in bed occasionally, just as everybody else does. But any container that is dry and draught-proof can be used, from an ordinary shopping basket or drawer for the smallest puppies, to packing cases or tea chests suitably chopped down and raised off the floor for the larger breeds.

Beds and bedding must be kept clean. Dogs like to hide bits of food and other objects in their beds. Small puppies not yet fully house-trained are frequent bedwetters. The base of the bedding can be made from a pile of old newspapers. On top of this place a couple of old rugs, blankets, cardigans, towels, or similar material. Choose a light-coloured material if you can. Its changing colour will remind you to wash it regularly. A blanket will begin to *look* dirty before the smell becomes too doggy. The newspapers can easily be thrown away and replaced each time.

Feeding

There are almost as many theories about feeding dogs as there are about feeding humans. At the very slight risk of causing widespread starvation among many household dogs, it is safe to say that today far more dogs are overfed than underfed. Missing a meal or two occasionally will do a fully-grown dog no harm at all. In fact, one well-known vet keeps one day in the week as a fasting day for all his dogs, and claims that they are all the healthier for it.

Puppies, of course, need small meals and plenty of them. Four meals a day are usually enough. Each meal should contain about $1\frac{1}{2}$ ounces of food. Meat should form about $\frac{1}{2}$ to $\frac{2}{3}$ of the complete ration. If your breeder has supplied a diet sheet for the first few months, follow that. If not, here is a general guide, but details vary according to the breed of dog.

Under 3 months, give a breakfast of lukewarm milk thickened with cereal and sweetened with glucose. This can be varied with beaten egg and soaked biscuits. A midday meal of sweetened milk or warm sweet tea, with a bit of puppy meal or some of the canned dog foods can be followed, at about 5 p.m., by the main meal of minced meat, raw or cooked. The bedtime meal should consist of lukewarm milk with a few hard biscuits to chew. As the puppy grows older you can leave out first the midday meal, and later the bedtime meal, increasing the amount of food in the other meals proportionately.

A fully grown dog should have a maximum of 2 meals a day. A snack for breakfast, followed by the main meal in the evening, is the usual routine. Meat is the staple diet. This can be raw or cooked, accompanied with a variety of vegetables, dog meal and biscuits. Some of the proprietary tinned dog foods are excellent, having, as they do, a balanced diet of vitamins. Keep sharp, easily splintered bones out of your pet's food. This includes chicken and fish bones. Large rounded bones are fine; they give a dog's jaws and teeth the exercise they need.

*   *   *

Don't pamper a dog with food. Snacks and titbits offered in between regular mealtimes can only lead to excess fat, faddiness, and eventual ill-health. If a dog leaves all or some of his food don't coax him to eat. Remove the food and let him wait until next feeding time. It goes without saying that feeding bowls should be kept scrupulously clean and any uneaten food should be thrown away after each meal. A bowl of drinking water should be available all the time.

The insides of a dog's ears are best cleaned with a soft rag moistened with surgical spirit. Other than that he should need very little grooming. His eyes may sometimes look a little runny. They may have been irritated by smoke, exhaust fumes, or grit. You need only wipe them gently dry at the corners. Inspect his claws from time to time to make sure that there are no sores developing between them. If there are, it may be a job for the vet.

Health

If your dog has not been inoculated by the breeder (who will give you a certificate to prove it if he has been), then you should go to a vet and arrange to have your puppy inoculated as soon as advisable. The inoculation gives protection from distemper and hepatitis. Although such inoculation is not guaranteed to give complete protection, it does mean that, should your dog unfortunately catch either disease in spite of being inoculated, the symptoms will be much milder and more easily treated.

In some countries inoculation against rabies is compulsory. Other ailments to which dogs are subject are the common human ones—colds, fever, constipation, and diarrhoea. Worms occur mainly in young puppies, and have been discussed in the earlier part of this chapter. Abscesses and canker are best treated by a vet.

House Training

Puppies, unlike kittens, do not have a natural instinct for going to the loo. They will relieve themselves whenever and wherever they feel like it. Unfortunately, they feel like it very often in the earliest weeks. If you are training your puppy indoors to begin with, place thick wads of newspaper near his bed. Try to get him to relieve himself in one particular spot each time, and praise him when he does so. Never on any account smack him or rub his nose in a mess. A puppy is not being naughty when such accidents occur, and he'll merely wonder why he is being punished. Once you can instil a sense of routine and regularity in your pet's mind, the battle is won. When it is time to get your puppy to use the garden, take him to the same place each time, repeating the process as you did with the newspapers. You may have to do this as many as 20 times a day. The most important times, of course, are first thing in the morning and last thing at night. Some puppies may not be able to contain themselves throughout a long night, but no animal deliberately fouls its own sleeping quarters.

Outdoor Training

A dog must learn good manners and obedience as soon as possible. This is not merely a social requirement, as it is with humans, but is so important that the dog's life itself may depend on it. As in all forms of training, patience is the main ingredient. Remember that your dog's main concern is to please you. If he succeeds, he is happy. He will soon interpret tones of praise and tones of displeasure. There is no need to use physical violence at any time. That can only result in a frightened or badtempered dog.

The first thing is to get your puppy to recognize his name. Use it repeatedly with all commands, and praise him when he responds. An intelligent dog will not take long to associate the word with his own identity. Simple commands like "sit", "stay", "lie down", "heel", and "walk" should then be given progressively. With a young puppy, these lessons should not last more than a few minutes at a time. The secret is little and often. A few minutes' instruction, twice a day, every day, will produce results far sooner than an hour every weekend would.

Before you take your puppy out into the strange world of pavements, pedestrians, and traffic, you will have to accustom him to wearing a collar and lead. Get him used to the collar first, without the lead. Legally, he is not allowed out on the streets without a collar that bears his owner's name and address. Start the puppy off with a light collar—one that is loose enough to be comfortable, but not loose enough for him to catch a paw in it. He will obviously do his best to get the thing off by scratching and biting at it. Fifteen minutes is long enough for him to endure the first feel of a collar. Increase the period each day until he actually begins to look forward to having the collar round his neck, and misses it when it is off. Then it is time to leave it on permanently. By this time the puppy should be about 8 to 10 weeks old. Harness type collars are not so effective at pulling a dog up short, and they sometimes tend to chafe his skin.

Once your dog is used to his collar, attach a lead to it. A fairly long leather lead is as good as any. Teach your dog to keep to heel by holding the lead in your right hand, with your dog on your left. This leaves your left hand free to control him by patting him, pressing him, or fondling as a reward for obedience. He will soon learn to walk in the same place without a lead. Similarly, the command "sit" should be accompanied by pressing down on his haunches, until he gets the idea and squats automatically whenever he hears the word, or reaches the kerb.

You will find many dog clubs where you can take your dog and train him under supervision, in the company of other owners with their dogs. One thing you must realize. A young dog cannot concentrate on anything for more than a few minutes at a time. Don't try to give him too much to do all at once, and wait until he has learned one rule before starting on another.

Apart from cleanliness about the house and general safety in the streets, there are the ordinary rules of good behaviour in and out of the house. Your dog should be trained not to attack other dogs in the street. It goes without saying that he should be safe with children and grown-ups. A biting dog can be destroyed by order of the courts. Similarly, a dog that is continually barking or whining or jumping up at visitors and guests can make you both extremely unpopular. It is really up to you and your training methods whether your dog is regarded as a public nuisance, or is a well-loved pet, welcomed wherever he goes.

Breeding
If you own a bitch, and wish to breed from her, you should select a stud well in advance, from breeders' ad-

vertisements. Your bitch will come into season for the first time when she is about 9 months old, and thereafter about every 6 months. For the first litter, you should let her be mated about the second or third time. For her health's sake she should not be allowed to have more than one litter a year. Four weeks after mating, a vet can tell whether the bitch is pregnant or not. When you know that she is carrying puppies, you should start giving her extra food from the sixth week.

It takes about 63 days from conception to birth. Gentle exercise is all that is required in the last days of the pregnancy. Your vet will advise you on any special precautions to be taken. At the time of the approaching birth you should provide a larger than usual box for your pet. If she is allowed to choose her own place for having the litter, it will probably be your bed. She will refuse all food a few hours before she has her pups. This is nothing to worry about.

A normal litter varies from about 4 to 8 pups. During the first few days you should leave the mother alone with her pups. She knows what is best for them. Keep her bedding clean and make sure that the whole family is kept warm. At this stage she needs no extra food or milk. After a few days, when the pups start suckling in earnest, milky foods should be increased. Don't pick up the pups too soon and too often. The mother may desert them altogether.

Puppies are born with their eyes tightly shut, but they should open normally after about 10 days. Weaning time varies, and is a gradual business. Once the pups start to climb in and out of their box they will also start to nibble at bits of food lying around. They will also lap milk and water from a saucer.

Your Dog and the Law

Every dog over 6 months old must have a licence. This can be obtained at any Post Office. As mentioned earlier, he must have his owner's name and address on his collar. It is a good plan to inscribe the dog's name too. This helps the authorities should he get lost or be involved in an accident. You will be held responsible for any damage your dog may cause, whether it is to property, to cattle, sheep, or poultry, or to other persons. The only exception to this is when it can be proved that the dog was acting in self-defence or in defence of you or your family and property. There are also a number of bye-laws that affect dogs: these vary from place to place. In some places it is an offence for a dog to foul the pavement. This emphasises the need for proper training and control.

Kinds of dogs

The following is a brief description of various kinds of dogs and their attributes. It does not pretend to be detailed nor comprehensive, but it may give you some idea of the kind of pet most suited to your needs.

Affenpinscher A shaggy black toy dog, whose prominent hairy chin earned it the name "monkey dog". 10 inches.

Afghan Hound An aristocratic-looking dog that was used in Afghanistan for hunting several thousand years ago. It is a good guard, and gentle with children, but needs lots of exercise and grooming. 25—29 inches.

Airedale The largest of the terriers, and a fine worker in and out of water. Strong, gentle with children, and faithful, it needs plenty of exercise. 23—24 inches.

Alaskan Malamute Often misnamed "Husky", it is used as a sledge dog. It can run for hours without tiring, and needs the exercise. 22 inches.

Alsatian The prince of guard dogs. Generally a one-man dog. Highly intelligent, it needs lots of exercise and proper training. Untrained it can be a killer. 22—26 inches.

Basenji A dog with a long history, originally from Egypt. It is known as a dog without a bark, but it does have a voice. It licks itself clean like a cat and occasionally bites unpredictably. 16—17 inches.

Basset Hound A popular pet, used in other days for hunting hares. It has a very large body with extremely short legs, and is affectionate and good with children, but needs exercise. 12—13 inches.

Beagle A hardy, active, affectionate dog looking like a small version of a Foxhound. Used for hare hunting, it is the smallest of the pack hounds. 12—16 inches.

Bedlington Terrier A long-legged, slender-bodied dog

with a soft, fleecy coat that makes it look like a lamb. Originally used for hunting badgers, today it makes an affectionate pet. 15—16 inches.

Belgian Tervueren A Belgian sheepdog resembling an Alsatian in build, but with a shaggy, mahogany-coloured coat. Affectionate and a good worker. 23 inches.

Bernese Mountain Dog Superficially resembles a Collie, but is jet black, with white chest and feet. Taken by Roman soldiers to Switzerland some 2,000 years ago, this breed was, until recently, almost unknown outside the Bernese Mountain area. Makes a loyal and affectionate pet. 20 inches.

Border Terrier One of the oldest breeds of terrier, originating in the north of England, and used to kill the powerful hill foxes. It has a wiry coat, and is essentially an active farm dog. 14 inches.

Borzoi An aristocratic, long-haired Russian wolfhound. It is related to the Greyhound and has become a symbol of expensive living. Gentle with children. 26—29 inches.

Boston Terrier A small, smooth-coated terrier, neat and finicky in appearance. It has a square head, with a snub nose. Properly fed and trained it makes a loyal and active pet. 12 inches.

Bouvier des Flandres Literally *Flemish cowherd*, this is a well-built, intelligent dog with a rough coat. It is powerful and active, and needs plenty of exercise. In Belgium it frequently has its ears trimmed and its tail cropped to enhance its appearance. 23—27 inches.

Boxer A medium to large, stocky, muscular dog, developed in Germany from the Bulldog and several terriers. It gets its name from its habit of striking out playfully with its front legs. An intelligent, loyal guard dog. 18—22 inches.

Bull Terrier A medium sized dog descended from the Bulldog and the Old White English Terrier. It has a wedgeshaped head, and a short, powerful body. It makes a good guard dog. 16 inches.

Bulldog The British national emblem. It is the result of a cross between the Mastiff and other breeds, produced in order to bait bulls. In spite of its fierce tradition it is gentle and reliable, but unusually subject to ailments. 15 inches.

Bullmastiff A noble dog, evolved from the Mastiff and the Bulldog, which was used widely by gamekeepers in the last century against poachers. May eat you out of house and home, but properly trained will protect that home unflinchingly. An untrained specimen can be lethal. 24—27 inches.

Cairn Terrier An ancient Scottish breed, cheerful and lively, this little dog is clean and docile indoors but a great ratter outside. Makes a good alarm dog. 9—10 inches.

Cavalier King Charles Spaniel A relatively new breed developed in the 1920s, this dog, although related to the King Charles Spaniel, is thought to resemble more closely the original 17th century breed. Lively and affectionate, although it tends to suffer from ear and eye trouble. 12 inches.

Chihuahua The smallest dog in the world. A tough little dog, originally from Mexico, where it hunts wild pig. Lively, intelligent, and affectionate, selective breading is making it so small that caesarian operations are becoming frequently necessary. 6—9 inches.

Chow Chow An ancient Chinese breed, with ruff and mane like a lion. Chows have blue tongues and surly expressions. They are one-man dogs and have a reputation for being aggressive with strangers. 20 inches.

Clumber Spaniel A heavy, short-legged hunting dog, with white coat and orange or lemon markings. Clumbers have good memories and are ideal dogs to train. 17—18 inches.

Cocker Spaniel Once a great gun dog, but now bred into a popular, brainless, but affectionate pet. Derived its name from its ability to flush woodcock from close cover. 16 inches.

Collie A wonderful sheepdog that exists in rough and smooth-haired versions. Extremely popular because it combines high intelligence with docility and loyalty. 22—24 inches.

Corgi A small Welsh dog, used to herd cattle. There are two breeds—the Pembroke, and the larger Cardigan. Both have short legs and deep, strong bodies. Corgis are friendly and intelligent. 11—13 inches.

Dachshund There are long and short-haired varieties of this brave and intelligent little dog. It is sometimes irreverently referred to as a *German sausage dog*, because of its long body and short legs. The German word means *badger dog*. 7—10 inches.

Dalmatian or *plum-pudding dog* White with black or liver-coloured blotches, this is a medium-sized dog with a noble face. Intelligent, and makes a good guard. 20 inches.

Dandie Dinmont Terrier About the size of a Dachshund, it gets its name from a character in Scott's novel, *Guy Mannering*. This active, courageous dog has large brown eyes, a shaggy coat, and a topknot on its forehead. 10 inches.

Deerhound A Scottish dog related to the Irish Wolfhound. A rugged, graceful dog, its keen eyesight can spot deer at great distances. Essentially an outdoor dog. 30 inches.

Dobermann A famous guard dog from Germany, with a reputation for treachery and ferocity. It can outfight most dogs, but its disposition depends on its training. 26 inches.

English Setter A large, handsome, graceful dog, with a keen sense of smell. A wonderful pet and superb gun dog. 26 inches.

Foxhound One of the oldest breeds of hounds, used for hunting foxes. Not recommended as a pet. 25 inches.

French Bulldog A smaller dog than the English version, with loose wrinkled skin on its face, a square head, and a body that is broader in front than behind. An affectionate and sturdy little dog. 12 inches.

Golden Retriever A beautiful, rather sad-looking, slimmer version of the Labrador. Needs plenty of grooming and exercise. 20—24 inches.

Gordon Setter A fine, methodical gun dog of medium size. It has a long, flat coat, and is easy to train. 23—27 inches.

Great Dane or *German Mastiff* An enormous dog, weighing 120 pounds, with appetite to match. Graceful, proud, and obedient, it makes a reliable watchdog. 30 inches.

Greyhound Allegedly the fastest dog in the world. It is a large dog, universally used for racing. Not suitable purely as a pet. 30 inches.

Griffon A medium-sized, wire-haired hunting dog, originally from The Netherlands. It has a keen sense of smell and is a wonderful retriever and pointer. 19—23 inches.

Griffon Bruxellois A toy dog with an appealing expression. It has a wiry, reddish brown coat (*griffon* means *thick-haired*) and a small, black, turned-up nose. Makes an affectionate pet. 9 inches.

Irish Setter A large, boisterous, graceful animal that makes an affectionate pet. It needs exercise and tends to be a one-owner animal. 25 inches.

Irish Terrier A wiry-haired, red or yellowish red, medium-sized dog. Noted for its fearless nature and devotion to its owner. A great ratter and a wonderful pet. 18 inches.

Irish Wolfhound The tallest of all dogs, it has a noble nature and a gargantuan appetite. An ancient breed, it allegedly died out at one time, and was revived about 100 years ago. 31—33 inches.

Japanese Spaniel A silky-haired, frisky little dog, related to the Pekinese. It has a very short nose, and a collar of long silky hairs round its neck. 10 inches.

Keeshond The Dutch national dog. It is related to the Chow Chow, Samoyed, and Pomeranian, and has slanting eyes marked with black lines that look like spectacles. 17—18 inches.

Kerry Blue Terrier A blue-grey dog that is sometimes called the national dog of Ireland. It is a wonderful ratter, and is also used to herd sheep and cows. It has a prominent beard and a forelock, usually combed down between its eyes. 18 inches.

King Charles Spaniel A toy dog that centuries ago came from China or Japan. It was a pet of the English nobility in the 1600s. It has a short, turned-up nose, and a thick, wavy, black and tan coat. Makes a playful and sentimental pet. 11 inches.

Labrador Retriever A popular and easily-trained gun dog that works particularly well in water. Its thick, water-resistant coat is usually black, but may be golden yellow. Makes a good guard dog and reliable pet. 22 inches.

Lakeland Terrier A compact, bold, alert dog that looks like a small Airedale. It was bred in the Lake District of England to hunt and kill foxes. An intelligent pet. 15 inches.

Maltese Probably the world's first lap dog. This toy breed was carried about by ancient Greek and Roman ladies 2,000 years ago. It has large black eyes and a long white coat that trails on the floor from a parting down the middle of its back. An extremely gentle and lovable pet. 7—10 inches.

Manchester Terrier A courageous little dog, bred to fight rats, badgers, and otters. It has a small head and a short coat, and makes a lively, interesting pet. 16 inches.

Mastiff A magnificent breed with a long history. It almost died out during World War II. The Romans imported the Old English Mastiff to fight lions in their circuses. It weighs 200 pounds and costs the earth to feed, but Mastiff owners rarely part with their pets. 30 inches.

Mexican Hairless A toy dog that has no coat. Its bare skin is warm to the touch, and was once superstitiously regarded as a cure for skin ailments. It has a narrow head and a pointed nose, with a little tuft of hair on its head. 11 inches.

Newfoundland Probably the best swimmer of all dogs. It is a large American breed, with a noble head and a dense, oily coat that keeps out the water. It can swim in the coldest water for hours, and is noted for its rescue of drowning persons. An even-tempered dog that makes a good watchdog. 28 inches.

Norwich Terrier A short-legged, bright-eyed, friendly little dog with a wiry coat. It is a good ratter and watchdog. First recognized as breed in 1932. 10—11 inches.

Norwegian Elkhound A compact hunting dog from Norway, it can pick up a scent more than 2 miles away. Makes a safe pet, but needs exercise and space. 20 inches.

Old English Sheepdog The largest of English sheep dogs. It peers out of an enormous shaggy coat of strong wool, developed to withstand the same weather as its charges. Intelligent, obedient, and full of fun. 22 inches.

Otterhound A rare breed with slightly webbed feet and a rough, oily coat. It looks a little like a shaggy Bloodhound. 24 inches.

Papillon A toy dog that gets its name from the French word for *butterfly*, with reference to its large, butterfly-shaped ears. It has a long silky coat and a plumed tail that it carries well over its back. An attractive little pet, believed to be related to the Chihuahua. 10 inches.

Pekinese The royal dog of China. This toy, in spite of its small size, is mischievous and brave. It has prominent eyes, bowed legs, and long-fringed ears. An excellent pet if not spoilt. 9 inches.

Pointer A short-haired gun dog, used to retrieve game birds. Its speed and keen sense of smell makes it valuable in the open country. It needs exercise, but is loyal and intelligent. 22 inches.

Pomeranian A tiny toy dog related to the Chow Chow and Samoyed. It has a sharp, pointed, fox-like face, a tail that curves over its back, and a penetrating bark. 9 inches.

Poodle A gay, lively, friendly, intelligent dog that is deservedly one of the world's most popular dogs. The three varieties are the *Toy,* the *Miniature,* and the *Standard.* Coats need to be professionally clipped in hot weather. 9—19 inches, according to variety.

Pug A popular toy dog originating in China. It is heavily built, with a short nose and a tightly curled tail. 10 inches.

Pyrenean Mountain Dog A large, very heavy dog, related to the St. Bernard. It is used as a sheep dog in the Pyrenees. It has heavy, long white hair that needs a lot of grooming. Makes a loyal and docile pet. 27—32 inches.

Rhodesian Ridgeback or *African Lion Dog* Bold and strong enough to hunt and hold a lion at bay, this breed has a distinctive hairy ridge down the middle of its back. A muscular, amenable, and very devoted dog. 25—27 inches.

Rottweiler A strong, stocky German cattle dog, with a fine sense of smell. It is also used as a police dog and makes a wonderful guard dog, but needs exercise. 25 inches.

St. Bernard An extremely valuable watch dog, guide dog, and pet, with a keen sense of smell. The St. Bernard's bulk and strength make it one of the world's heaviest dogs—up to 250 pounds. In spite of its size it is very gentle. 24 inches.

Saluki Probably the oldest breed of dog in the world, having been traced back some 9,000 years. Related to the Greyhound, it is one of the fastest dogs. Its beautiful feathery coat needs constant grooming. 23—28 inches.

Samoyed From northern Siberia, it is used to pull sledges and guard reindeer herds. It is one of the oldest breeds of domesticated dogs, and always seems to be smiling. 20 inches.

Schnauzer A German terrier, for many hundreds of years used to herd cattle. It is a keen, high-spirited, powerfully-built dog that comes in three sizes: Miniature (14 inches), Standard (19 inches), and Giant (24 inches).

Scottish or *Aberdeen Terrier* A sturdy, fearless little dog, sometimes called the "die-hard". It has short legs, a large head, and a harsh coat, generally black or black-brindle. 10 inches.

Sealyham Terrier So-called because it was bred at Sealyham, in Wales, about 1850. Trained to follow rats, foxes, and badgers to earth, it has short legs and a powerful body. Its blunt, heavy muzzle encloses powerful jaws. 10 inches.

Shetland Sheepdog or *Sheltie* One of the most beautiful of all dogs. A miniature version of the Collie it has the same type and colour of coat, needing a lot of grooming. It makes a wonderful playmate and guard. 12 inches.

Siberian Husky An Arctic sledge dog related to the Samoyed. Graceful and alert, in spite of its great strength, the Husky makes a reliable and obedient guard dog. 23 inches.

Skye Terrier A tiny, spirited dog that will attack a rat not much smaller than itself. The hair on its head veils its eyes. Great fun to own. 8 to 10 inches.

Springer Spaniel A gun dog that looks like a larger, heavier version of the Cocker Spaniel. Its thick water-and-thorn-resistant coat can be of various colours. It has an appealing nature and makes an excellent pet. 20 inches.

Staffordshire Bull Terrier A distant relative of the ordinary

Bull Terrier, this dog was bred by Staffordshire miners purely to fight other dogs. With its deep chest and square stance, it resembles an oldtime prizefighter. Very good as a guard dog. 15 inches.

West Highland White Terrier The only all-white Scottish terrier, it carries it tail held high and its ears cocked. Bright, alert eyes confirm its intelligence. It makes a faithful pet. 11 inches.

Whippet A swift, lean, muscular dog, that looks like a small Greyhound. It has a pointed head and a long, tapering tail. It is often used for hunting rabbits and for racing. Whippets are very fine watch-dogs. 18 inches.

Yorkshire Terrier A gentle, docile toy dog, but on occasion bold enough to kill a rat. It is small enough to be carried in a pocket. Its long, silky hair touches the ground and needs frequent combing and drying. 8 inches.

Dogs

Bulldog

Spaniel

Old English
Sheepdog

Poodle

Alsatian

Dachshund

Cats

Cats are the smallest members of the family that includes tigers, jaguars, and lions. They are probably descended from a weasel-like animal that lived about 55 million years ago. About 40 million years ago, the cat as we know it today began to appear. The domestic cat probably evolved from three different species: the Kaffir cat, the African wild cat, and the European wild cat.

The ancient Egyptians were the first people known to have domestic cats. These cats became so useful in keeping rodents out of their vast grain stores that the Egyptians valued them highly, and even worshipped them. One of their godesses had the head of a cat. The ancient Romans looked on cats as the symbols of liberty. Phoenician traders probably carried Egyptian cats to Europe where they bred with the European wild cat and produced the domestic cat that we see today in its many varieties.

Few people are indifferent to cats. They either hate and fear them (a small minority this) or else they adore them. Cats make unique pets. They are playful and affectionate but at the same time they retain a dignity, an independence that cannot be bought or coaxed. A cat has many virtues and few drawbacks. It is a swift and graceful mover, but can be warm and cuddly. It is unobtrusive but beautiful to look at. It is fastidiously clean. It is comparatively noiseless. It can be cheap and easy to buy, and inexpensive to feed and look after. Kittens, and even some adult cats, are the most playful things in the world, and make ideal pets for children.

Buying
Unless you are going to breed your own cats and/or exhibit them, there is no sound reason for investing in a pedigree animal. Non-pedigree cats have all the virtues of their more exalted sisters and may be a good deal hardier, but of course they will never have quite the right markings or exact shape required for the show ring.

Pedigree cats can cost anything from 3 to 30 guineas. There are always plenty of them for sale in the adver-

tisements in the various cat and pet magazines. If you go
to one of the many cat shows you can see the different
breeds being exhibited, and make your choice from them.

Whatever kind of cat you buy, there are certain points
you should look for. An alert, aggressive kitten, with
bright eyes and a fearless attitude is the one most likely
to succeed in becoming a healthy, well-adjusted pet. Its
nose should be moist (but not running), and its coat soft.
If the kitten looks too fat, or has a patchy or harsh coat,
it may be suffering from some fairly mild and temporary
ailment that it will soon surmount. Or it may, of course,
have been improperly fed. But in any case it is best not to
take risks with an off-colour kitten. There are so many
available in perfect health that there is absolutely no need
to handicap yourself by having to nurse an ailing animal
from the start.

If you are not going to breed from your cat for exhibition
or profit, by all means have it neutered, whether it is a
tom or a *queen*. With toms, the operation is a simple one,
which the vet will perform for a small fee. A tom that is
not castrated will eventually grow into a battling Romeo
who will use your home merely as a hotel for resting
between frequent bouts of fighting and amorous conquest.
He will spray over your furniture, announce his presence
with objectionable smells, rend the night with his cries,
and stand a good chance of being run over during his
nightly visits to neighbouring gardens.

Once neutered, a queen will require no supervision to

prevent her bearing 3 litters a year every year until she is worn out. There will be no danger of finding litters born in your bed, or on your best sofa; you will not have to put up with your queen's calling every three weeks until she is mated; and you will not be faced with an agonizing choice between having the house overrun with kittens or having to destroy most or all of them.

The neutering of a queen is a complex operation, requiring a full anaesthetic. It also costs more. Your vet will decide the best time to do it. Some experts prefer to let a queen have one litter before she is neutered. Contrary to many beliefs, neutered toms and queens do not degenerate after their operation. They become home-loving, affectionate towards human beings, hygienic, and serene. They do not put on too much weight, provided they are fed properly. Their general health improves. Toms do not bear the scars and abscesses of battle, and the queens' coats become thick and shiny with the extra care they are able to devote to themselves.

A kitten should be at least 8 weeks old—that is, properly weaned—before being removed from its mother. It is by then showing some of the independence that is the hallmark of all cats. Give it the run of your home, warmth and security, and with its inborn streak of curiosity it will quickly settle down in its new surroundings.

Housing
No pet will make fewer demands on its owner for attention than a cat. This applies to housing and bedding as

well as to its other needs. It appreciates care and attention, but if these are lacking it rather sadly keeps itself to itself and gets along quite well without them. A box or basket for the new kitten, lined with newspapers and an old rug or woollen scarf, is ideal. Keep it in a warm room, away from draughts.

If you have no garden handy you will have to supply a shallow metal tray, filled with earth, cinders, or torn-up paper, for sanitary purposes. Every time it shows signs of wanting to relieve itself, put the kitten on it. It will learn where its duty lies within hours. Keep the tray cleaned every day, adding a little mild disinfectant from time to time. If you do have a garden, put the kitten in the same part of it each time and again, it will be quick to learn. Cats are fastidiously clean animals and you should have no trouble with your kitten in this respect after the first few days.

Feeding

At the age of 8 or 9 weeks your kitten must have four meals a day. Little and often should be your motto, as with most young animals. Vary the diet as much as you can. Cats have surprising likes and dislikes in the food line, and also vary widely in the amounts they eat. But a kitten is rarely greedy in the sense that a young puppy is. It will generally stop eating as soon it feels it has had enough. Four heaped tablespoonfuls of food a day should be sufficient for the young kitten. You can always increase or decrease the amount slightly according to whether your pet obviously wants more or is leaving food uneaten.

A typical menu might be:

Breakfast and teatime — a tablespoonful of cereal in warm milk, slightly sweetened.

Lunch and supper — some scraped raw meat, or shredded boiled fish in milk, with a few chopped raw greens.

Milk should always be part of your pet's diet, but it does not replace water for drinking. Fresh water should always be available. Never leave the remains of one meal to serve as part of the next. All cats require some "roughage"— that is, hard foods on which they can exercise their teeth and jaws. There are a number of excellent proprietary food tablets on the market that serve this purpose, and also stimulate digestion. Cats also need grass. If you do not have daily access to a garden, a little grass grown indoors in a plant pot is adequate.

When your kitten is about 4 months old, cut the meals down to 3 a day, but increase the quantities to make up for the missing meal. When it is full-grown it needs only 2 meals a day—morning and evening. Again, the quantities should be increased experimentally until you discover what constitutes a satisfying amount. Variations in diet can include cooked root-vegetables, raw minced meat, cooked rabbit, fish, liver, some of the reputable tinned cat foods, and occasionally a few drops of halibut or cod liver oil. The odd yeast tablet, to stimulate appetite, and an occasional drop of medicinal paraffin to free hair balls that may be impeding digestion, are possible additions to the menu. But feeding is largely a matter of common sense. Provided the meals are trotted out regularly at approximately the same time each day, and provided they are clean and fit for cat (or even human!) consumption, you should have no trouble at all.

Grooming

Because cats are such naturally clean and particular animals, little manual care is necessary. Regular brushing and combing of long-haired cats will ensure that hairs are not left all over your carpets and furniture. Loose hairs are also sometimes swallowed and form hair balls inside the cat. Manual grooming will reduce this risk, and will also improve the sheen and condition even of short-haired cats. Never bathe your cat if you can possibly avoid it. Although cats are strong swimmers, most of them hate water and will usually use it only for drinking purposes.

A thorough dusting with any one of the many excellent flea powders available should quickly rid the fur of unwelcome visitors, if you suspect that they are there.

*   *   *

When your cat "sharpens his claws" on your best furniture he is actually exercising his muscles and helping to shed the removable covering on his claws. This is a natural function. It should not be suppressed—merely transferred. A scratching post in the garden, or a board in the house with a piece of old carpet nailed to it will do admirably. When shown this alternative your cat will soon prefer it to the furniture.

Health

If your kitten has not been inoculated against feline infectious enteritis, have it done as soon as possible, otherwise you may be sentencing it to death. It is a horrible disease, highly infectious, and once under way is very difficult to cure. Inoculation provides complete immunity. Another disease that is serious though not necessarily fatal, is feline distemper—or cat flu, as it is sometimes called. No certain immunization has yet been discovered, but warmth and loving nursing will usually pull the animal through.

Apart from these two ailments, cats are remarkably healthy. Many cats suffer from wounds inflicted by other cats or dogs, and these should be taken to the vet if they look at all serious. Hunting cats, such as those found on farms, sometimes suffer from worms. These can be expelled when treated by any of various worming agents on the market.

Ear canker can be a persistent source of trouble. If your cat keeps on scratching its ear, or continually rubs its head, examine its ears. The canker is caused by a parasite. There are a number of drugs that will eliminate the trouble, but in any case, careful swabbing inside the ear with cottonwool will ensure cleanliness.

Never give your cat any preparations that contain either D.D.T. or castor-oil; both are poisonous to cats. Finally, if in doubt about your cat's health, do take him to the vet. Although cats may be healthier than most domestic

animals, they seem to succumb more easily to the few
diseases they do contract, and many expire while their
owners are wondering if they are ill or not.

Breeding
A litter of kittens is an endearing sight, and gives hours
of pleasure and amusement. If you have a mongrel queen,
and want kittens—relax. She will find her own mate without any help from you, when she is ready. The difficulty
lies in preventing a pedigree queen from mating with any
casual tom.

A pregnant queen needs little extra care or attention. Milk
and food should be increased towards the end of her
pregnancy, and while she is nursing. Weeks before the
kittens are due (gestation takes 65 days) she will start
sleeping in a particular place, making it quite evident that
that is where she intends to have her litter. If this place
happens to be your bed, alternative accommodation should
be lovingly but firmly offered. Many cats choose dark,
warm, secluded cupboards. In that case, all you have to
do is to provide a large draughtproof box filled with
plenty of newspaper and some old rags. When the time
comes, leave your queen alone. She will generally be able
to cope without trouble, cleaning the new-born kittens
herself immediately. Should she be crying and in obvious
difficulty, a kitten may have got stuck. Call the vet.

Newly born kittens are about the size of mice, completely
helpless, and with eyes shut tight. They open their eyes
after about 10 days. Once all the kittens are born, place

some water and milk within easy reach of the mother, so that she has to move as little as possible. If she has to leave her babies repeatedly at first, she may eventually leave them altogether. Do not handle the kittens any more than you have to, but decide promptly how many you intend to keep. Surplus kittens should be taken to the vet to be destroyed (if they cannot be given away as pets). Don't try to do the job yourself, and don't take all the kittens away from the mother at once. This is cruel, mentally and physically. Excess milk that is produced will cause the mother much pain if she has no kittens to suckle.

After 2 or 3 weeks the kittens will start to stagger rather shakily about the box and do their best to climb out of it. Once they are on their feet you can start to wean them. Sweetened baby-milk food is better than cow's milk, so start them on that. They will still be taking some milk from their mother, but she will gradually discourage them as she feels the nip of their growing teeth. You can also start giving them a little raw, scraped, lean meat. Vary this with a bit of cooked rabbit or beaten raw egg. The mother will generally teach them to lap from a saucer or a spoon. At about eight weeks they should be fully weaned.

The procedure for breeding pedigree cats is the same, except for the choice of a mate. A queen will come into her first season, and start calling, at about 6 months. From then on, until she is out of season, she must be kept well out of reach of prowling toms—and there will be plenty

of them! It could be kinder and healthier to let her wait
for her second or third season before mating her. She will
then be sexually and physically mature. She usually comes
into season every 4 or 5 weeks, and the season lasts for
about 7 days at a time. But these times are only approx-
imate, and vary with individual animals. The choice of
stud is up to you. If you can, you should consult the
breeder who sold you the queen. Otherwise, any reputable
cat-breeder will advise you. Stud bookings must be made
well in advance, and the fee can be several guineas. If by
any chance your queen escapes, and is mated by a mongrel
tom before you can get her to a pedigree stud, don't
despair. If she gives birth to a mongrel litter, this won't
prevent her from producing pedigree kittens from a sub-
sequent mating with a pedigree tom.

Kinds of cats

More than 30 pedigree breeds and varieties are officially
recognized for registration purposes by the Governing
Council of the Cat Fancy. They are divided into two main
groups—Long-Haired and Short-Haired.

Long-Haired Cats These were produced by the inter-
breeding of Persian and Angora cats. They have wide,
intelligent foreheads, large, round eyes, short legs, and
bushy tails. They are generally more dignified and quiet
than the short-haired breeds. They are not so quick or
lithe in their movements and prefer to sit around and look
decorative. They give their owners rather more work to do

because their long silky fur is always improved by extra grooming. Popular varieties are the *"Blue Persian"* with its puggish nose and smokey grey fur; the *Chinchilla,* all white, with black-rimmed, blue eyes; and the *Tortoiseshell,* with a variety of colours seemingly splashed haphazardly all over its coat. Incidentally, male Tortoiseshells are a rarity. White cats with blue eyes are commonly deaf. Potential buyers should test a kitten by clapping suddenly behind it, and noting if it reacts.

Short-Haired Cats These are subdivided into Orientals and others. The others are called British in Britain, European on the continent of Europe, and Domestic in America. Orientals have lithe bodies, pointed heads, almond-shaped eyes, and long, tapering tails. They have distinctive characters of their own and take readily to a leash. They love travelling, and are more like a cross between a dog and a monkey than the conventional idea of a cat. Of these, probably the best known is the *Siamese.* Highly intelligent, affectionate, and loyal, the Siamese still has certain drawbacks. Chief among these is its cry, which is long and wailing. One way of overcoming this handicap is to keep a pair. Siamese love to accompany their owners for walks. They are playful and mischievous, but at times can be off-puttingly independent. There are several varieties of Siamese cats. They are classified according to the colour of their *points* (ears, face, feet, and tail). *Seal point* cats have cream-coloured bodies with dark brown points and clear blue eyes. *Blue points* have whitish bodies with greyish blue points. *Chocolate points* and *lilac points* are other recognized varieties.

Another well-known short-haired cat is the *Russian Blue.*
A blue-grey cat, with soft, short, plush-like fur, it has a
narrow, wedge-shaped head and large ears. Russian Blues
have long, muscular bodies and long nimble legs. They
move gracefully and have rather quiet voices. The *Burmese* has a solid seal-brown coat, with slanting, golden
yellow eyes. Its body is slim and its tail long.

A sensitive Oriental breed is the *Abyssinian,* which
probably originated in Egypt. It is a medium-sized cat
with a tawny brown coat, each hair being tipped with
black. It is a fine boned cat, with a rather wild air about
it. Its eyes are green or hazel and it has a soft miaow. It
seems to require rather more affection from its owners
than most cats, but will repay this with undivided loyalty.

Other short-haired cats, apart from the Orientals, include
Black, White, Blue, Tortoiseshell, Cream, and various
Tabbies. A unique short-haired cat is the *Manx.* This
breed lived originally in the Isle of Man. True Manx cats
are completely tailless. Their hindlegs are much longer
than their front legs so that when they run they adopt an
almost rabbit-like, hopping gait. They are extremely tough
cats, and can run faster and further than most other
domesticated cats.

A fairly recent mutation is the *Rex* cat, which appeared
originally in Devon and Cornwall. These, too, are unique
in being practically hairless. These so-called "naked cats"
command high prices but are pathetically ill-equipped to
survive anything but the mildest of winters.

Cats
Abyssinian

Persian

Siamese

Short
Haired

POPULAR RODENTS

Rabbits and hares

The origin of the rabbit is somewhat obscure, but it is known that rabbits were kept by the Romans in 120—130 A.D. The wild rabbit—from which the domesticated breeds are derived—was not introduced into Britain until the 1100s.

Rabbits in this country were first bred for their meat and fur. They were kept by landowners in large enclosures called *warrens*. It was not until the 1700s that domestic rabbits were kept as they are today. It was about this time that the first few fancy breeds began to appear.

Today, there are many different breeds of rabbits. Some have long hair, some short, some are bred for their meat, while others are bred for their fur. When buying a pet rabbit, you have a wide selection to choose from.

There is much to be said for keeping rabbits as pets. They are clean and safe to handle, cheap to feed and easy to look after. You can breed rabbits for exhibition or for selling stock, and perhaps make a profit from your hobby.

Anyone wishing to keep rabbits as anything other than pets should read the rabbit breeder's own magazine, *Fur and Feather*. It not only provides a wealth of information about breeding and exhibiting, but its advertising columns provide a means of both buying and selling stock.

But the rabbit kept as a pet will provide its owner with a great deal of interest and amusement.

Kinds of rabbits

Choosing a rabbit will depend largely on whether you intend to go in for exhibiting or breeding, or merely for keeping it as a pet. The different breeds of rabbits are so numerous that it would be impossible to attempt to cover them all in this book, but here are a few of the more popular breeds.

The *Dutch* is perhaps more frequently kept as a pet than any other. It is a marked breed, its fur being white and another colour. Of the 8 different colours available, the 2 most popular are black and blue.

The *English,* like the Dutch, is a very common pet. Again, it is a marked breed—white with blue, black, tortoiseshell, chocolate, or grey markings.

Both the English and the Dutch breeds are exhibited. Being marked, and judged on their markings, they can be picked out for their quality while still in the nest.

Following the Dutch and English in popularity is the *Netherland Dwarf.* This breed rarely weighs more than 2 1/4 pounds as an adult, and is bred only for exhibition purposes. It does, however, make an excellent pet for a small child, due to its compactness and ease of handling.

The *Angora,* which is probably one of the oldest known breeds of domestic rabbit, is kept for its wool. It is very distinctive in appearance, because its fur is long, fine, and soft, and stands well out from its body. It is the only rabbit from which wool can be obtained.

Although normally white, the Angora can be bred in as many as 12 colours. It makes a beautiful pet and is very successful in exhibitions. However, before buying an Angora remember that, because of its fine coat, it requires considerably more attention than other breeds.

The *Chinchilla,* like the Angora, is an extremely popular exhibition animal. Normally bred for its fur, it is nevertheless often kept as a pet. Unlike the Angora, it has short hair, and is therefore a lot easier to look after.

Other popular breeds are *New Zealand, Whites, Tans, Sables,* and *Lops*.

Feeding

Looking after rabbits is not really a problem. They should be fed twice a day—morning and evening—and should always have fresh drinking water available to them. Their meals should be made up of wet and dry foods. Wet foods can be either mashes made up with cereals and boiled vegetables, bread, and milk—or green foods such as cabbage, lettuce, or clover. Dry foods can be cereals, biscuits, bread crusts, or special brands of rabbit food as sold in pet shops. Variety in feeding is very important, because what some foods lack can be made up in others. This gives the rabbit a balanced diet.

* * *

Rabbits should be fed at regular intervals. A hungry rabbit will not be able to make the best use of its food, and restlessness caused by having to wait for its food will result in the waste of much energy.

* * *

Apart from normal meals, hay can be left in the hutch at all times. This will provide roughage. Certain types of hay contain extra protein. Clover hay and nettle hay, because of their high protein content, are the most popular among rabbit keepers.

Handling
When handling rabbits, any form of grip should be gentle but firm. If the rabbit feels insecure it will struggle and may damage both itself and the handler.

There are many ways of picking up a rabbit. Perhaps the most popular method is to take hold of the ears close to the head with one hand while lifting the rabbit from underneath with the other. The hand holding the ears restrains the animal while the other hand takes the weight. Rabbits should never be lifted by the ears alone.

Another way to pick up a rabbit is to take it by the loose skin over its shoulders with one hand, and to use the other hand to lift it from beneath. Again, the hand holding the skin is only there to balance and restrain the animal, while the other hand takes all the weight.

Housing
Rabbits are naturally active animals. They should therefore be given as large a hutch as possible. Hutches are generally made of wood, with the front enclosed partly by wood and partly by wire. The part covered by wood gives protection from the damp and cold.

The hutch can be kept out of doors all the year round, providing it is wind and waterproofed. Rabbits can stand cold weather but not dampness.

For the floor of the hutch, you should use some form of tray. This will make cleaning a lot easier. The floor should be covered with either sawdust or peat moss, and the sleeping quarters filled with straw or hay.

Hutches should be cleaned out at least twice a week, or if possible, every day. Rabbits are very clean animals and will not smell if properly looked after.

If you have a walled or securely fenced garden, you can let your rabbit out for exercise. If this is not possible, you can always construct a run, fenced in with wire netting. Your rabbit will benefit from this, and will in turn help you by keeping the grass short.

Breeding

Rabbits will reach maturity, depending on the size of the breed, in 2 to 6 months. However, they should not be allowed to breed until they are at least 6 months old—or, in the case of larger breeds, 9 months.

The *doe* (female) should be placed in the *buck's* (male's) cage. After mating she should be returned to her own cage and left for a week. She should then again be placed with the buck. If the mating was successful the doe will refuse the buck and should be returned to her own hutch. The gestation period is normally 31 days; but young born between 28 and 34 days from mating will usually be healthy. During pregnancy the doe should be provided with seperate nesting quarters in her hutch. She should not be handled, and should be disturbed only for cleaning purposes. About a week before the young are due, the doe will build a nest from the straw in her sleeping quarters, which she will line with fur from her breast. This nest should not be disturbed for any reason.

From the start of the pregnancy, meals should be increased from 2 to 3 a day. As soon as the doe starts to build, fresh bread and milk should be given daily. This should continue until the young are large enough to fend for themselves.

Following the birth of the young, they should be left alone for at least 5 days. After this time, gently remove the mother and inspect the litter. If you find there are more than 6 in the litter, remove the smallest, and either place them with another doe with a smaller litter or destroy them. This will ensure the survival and fitness of the remainder of the litter.

The young are born blind, and with very little fur. After 10 days, their eyes will open, and after 3 weeks they will make short excursions from the nest.

At the end of that time, you should remove the mother to another hutch. The young should then be left together until they are 3 months old, when the bucks should be separated from the does. Sexing rabbits is rather difficult, especially for the novice. The easiest method is to hold the animal upside down and draw back the fur around the sexual organ. In the buck, it will appear to protrude slightly as a rounded tip, while in the doe the organ appears slit-like and slopes back towards the tail. Generally the organ of the buck is placed further from the tail than that of the doe.

From the time that the mother and litter are separated, the young should be given, in addition to their normal food, a moist mash of water, milk, and cereal or biscuits three times a day.

Health

Kept clean and dry, rabbits will generally remain healthy. They may, however, suffer from some of the more common ailments.

Too much grain and not enough greenstuffs will cause constipation, which can be cured by increasing the green food in the diet. If this is not successful, a little Glauber salts added to the drinking water will soon help.

Rabbits that sneeze and have constantly running noses are probably suffering from a disease commonly known as "*snuffles*". This is a very infectious disease, so affected animals must be kept away from other rabbits in order to prevent the disease spreading. It has to be treated by a vet, who will probably prescribe an antibiotic.

Among the parasitic diseases that attack rabbits, the most common is *coccidiosis*. This is caused by a parasite living in the intestines, liver, or brain of the animal. The first symptom of the disease is diarrhoea. The infected animal will pass the eggs of the parasite with its droppings, which can easily lead to other rabbits becoming affected. The best way to combat coccidiosis is to keep everything so clean that the disease cannot spread, and must therefore die out.

If your rabbit continually shakes its head, it may have ear canker. This takes the form of scabs inside the ears. If caught early, this can be cleared up by frequent dusting of the infected parts with flowers of sulphur. But if the sores start to spread a vet should be consulted.

As well as ear canker, rabbits will occasionally develop sores around the vent and genitals. These cases should be treated by swabbing with a mild disinfectant, then drying and wiping over with an ointment.

Exhibiting

Exhibiting rabbits is an interesting and often profitable hobby. If you intend to keep rabbits for exhibiting, you should start by visiting rabbit club shows. *Fur and Feather* lists forthcoming shows, at which the novice can learn to recognize the different breeds he would like to keep himself. Rabbit shows also provide a means for the beginner to contact fanciers who sell stock.

Exhibiting rabbits, or the *Rabbit Fancy*, as it is known, is a well supported pastime. Most clubs are affiliated to the British Rabbit Council, which is the central governing body of the Rabbit Fancy.

Local rabbit clubs meet fairly regularly and provide such amenities as discussions on rabbit topics, lectures, social events, and of course, shows.

There are many types of rabbit shows, the most frequent being the table shows held by the local rabbit clubs. These are usually 1-day events.

As well as the local table shows there are also several Championship Shows. These may be special rabbit shows, such as the Bradford Championship Show, or events like the Dairy Show at which there is a large rabbit section.

Prizes consist of prize cards and money, prize cards usually going to the first 7 places in any class, and money to the first 3 or 4 places.

Rabbits for showing have to be in first class condition. A really good animal may easily be classed below a not so good one because of its condition. A show rabbit should have no moult and its coat should be in immaculate condition.

This "finish" is often the deciding factor between two rabbits on the judging table.

The best way to prepare a rabbit is by grooming or brushing it with your hand. This method clears dust and dead hairs, and provides a fine polished finish.

White breeds of rabbit need somewhat more attention. To keep them clean they must live in spotless hutches, because hutch stains will not only spoil a rabbit but are difficult to remove.

Dirty spots on white rabbits can be erased by rubbing with a piece of bread. French chalk, talcum powder, or surgical spirit can also be used.

Certain breeds have to be trained to show themselves to

the greatest advantage. For example, the Polish rabbit should be taught to sit on its haunches to show itself off to the judge; the Belgian Hare should "pose" well to show off its shape, and the Flemish Giant should sit in a position to show the greatest length. Regular handling by the owner should ensure the quietness and good behaviour of a rabbit on the exhibition table.

The best place for the beginner to start exhibiting is at one of the local table shows. Having applied to the local club secretary for details of the show and lists of classes, he can then decide on the appropriate class for which his rabbit can be entered.

The classes of rabbit shows are of 2 kinds: straight breed classes, and duplicate classes. Straight breed classes are for particular breeds, such as Dutch, English, etc. These classes are often subdivided according to age or sex. Thus classes may be Dutch adult, Dutch adult doe, Dutch under 4 months, etc.

The duplicate classes are of great variety, and include such things as the Breeders class (in which any breed may be entered as long as it was bred by the exhibitor). The Novice Exhibit (one in which only animals that have never taken a first prize may be entered), and challenge classes for all comers.

Rabbits can be exhibited by their owners at shows, or sent by rail to shows in different parts of the country. If your rabbit has to travel any distance to a show, particular attention should be paid to its travelling box. This should be well ventilated, and should contain plenty of clean, dry bedding. Bad ventilation and dirty bedding will spoil the condition of the rabbit and lessen its chances in exhibition.

An adequate supply of food should also be made available to a rabbit while travelling. The food provided, however, should not mark or stain the rabbit.

Once at the show the rabbit will be checked in, and a small gummed tag will be attached to its ears for recognition. It will then be placed in a pen.

When the time comes for judging, the rabbit will be taken from the pen by a steward and placed on a table before the judges. It is obvious, therefore, that your rabbit must be used to being handled if it is to remain calm at the show.

Different breeds of rabbits are judged on their own special points, and although judges are aware of what constitutes the best exhibits, some will give more weight to particular points than others. For example, in the *Rex* breed, one judge may like a fine silky coat, whereas another judge may consider density of hair to be more important. Therefore, by taking note of the preferences of different judges, the exhibitor is able to place his entries before a judge who is favourable to the points displayed by his exhibits.

To ensure consistent success, the fancier has to have a very thorough knowledge of the breed he exhibits. He must be able to recognize and cultivate all the finer points of his exhibits through meticulous care and attention. He must also ensure that his animals are always kept in the best possible condition, and arrive safely at the judging table in the same state. All the present domestic breeds of rabbits have been evolved due to the stimulus of rabbit shows. These shows, apart from providing the fancier with a great deal of pleasure, and often excitement, have brought rabbit fanciers together and have led to the standardizing of the different breeds and the formation of an ideal for each breed.

Hares

Leverets, as the offspring of hares are called, are difficult to find in the shops, but fairly easy to obtain in the country, if you know where to look. A mother hare will leave her young in *forms* (hollows) in clumps of nettles or rushes, by the edges of copses and similar places. She goes at intervals to each form in turn, to suckle the leverets. These rely entirely on camouflage for protection, and can actually be picked up without their attempting to get away.

Although hares have been hand-reared successfully, and their owners have spoken volumes for them, they have so many disadvantages that they cannot really be recommended as pets. In the first place, you have to acquire the animal at just the right age: too young and it will die on your hands; too old and it becomes sulky, uncooperative, and vicious.

*   *   *

Hares by nature are stupid, panicky creatures, and take to captivity less kindly than most animals. If you provide too large an enclosure for them they tend to dash around wildly and injure themselves. And to cage such an active animal in a tiny hutch is cruel in the extreme and should never be done.

Hamsters, cavies and chinchillas

Hamsters are small rodents, about 6 inches long (including a stumpy tail), which are closely related to mice and squirrels. Their history is interesting. Several species of wild hamster have been known to zoologists for two or three hundred years. They are about 12 inches long and inhabit various parts of Europe and North Asia. But the golden hamster is found only near Aleppo, in Syria, and is not commonly seen even there. This breed was first discovered and reported in that area in 1839, but it was not until nearly a century later, in 1930, that a female with a litter of 12 was discovered in a burrow, and sent to Jerusalem for scientific examination. The family bred well in captivity and pairs were eventually sent to Europe, Britain, and the United States. Every one of the millions of golden hamsters that are kept as pets all over the world today are believed to have descended from that original captive family of a mother and her 12 babies.

The word "hamster" is an adaptation of the German word *hamsterer*, which means "hoarder". The hamster has earned this description because of its habit of hoarding food. In the wild it lives in a complicated series of burrows, generally carved out in grain fields. When gathering food in these fields, the animals store what they cannot eat in large pouches on either side of the head, extending from their upper cheeks to their shoulders. They then carry the pouched food to their burrows, where it is kept for the winter, when food is hard to come by.

Hamsters, when adult, weigh 3 to 5 ounces. They have a short cobby body, and black, rather prominent, beady eyes. The coat is dense, golden brown above shading off into grey or white underneath. There are some black markings on the head.

Hamsters make ideal pets, especially where space is at a premium, as they can be kept even in a tiny flat. They are clean, healthy, do not have the characteristic rodent smell, are cheap to feed and keep, and are endearing and entertaining creatures to watch, once they have been tamed.

Buying
You should be able to pick up a specimen of the common variety of golden hamster at almost any pet shop for a few shillings. If you are not interested in breeding your own hamsters, a young male about 6 or 7 weeks old is your best pet. Look for a firm, dense coat, and alert, bright eyes. Examine the ears and nose for pimples and scabs. If you find any evidence of these, pass on to another animal. In an animal as young as this, the fur tends to be greyish rather than golden. The hamster turns browner as it grows older.

Handling
The hamster is a timid animal with sharp teeth. Because it is so small it needs very careful handling. The correct way to pick it up is to place one hand over its back with your fingers curled round its body. If a child's hand is too small to cope safely with this manoeuvre, the other hand should be placed under the animal's tummy for support. The more the hamster is handled, the tamer it will become, and the more entertaining it will be to watch. An adult specimen, unused to human hands, may bite in panic at first, and although bites are painful they are never poisonous. Move slowly and gently. Avoid loud noises, and approach your pet with some tit-bit on the palm of your hand until he has gained complete confidence and trust. You can then let him out of his cage and give him the run of your room—provided it is hamster-proof! At the first opportunity he will disappear through a crack in the door, a hole in the floor boards, or through the half open window. The chances of finding him again, before

a passing cat or dog does, are slim. Once he has accepted you he will run all over you, investigating everything minutely. He can even be taught to beg for his food and perform simple tricks.

Housing

Hamsters are solitary and aggressive little creatures. Stags and does will fight viciously except at the actual moment of mating. Even animals of the same sex will fight when adult. Stags are generally slightly smaller and more docile than does. If you are keeping more than one hamster you will have to provide separate cages for each of them. Hamsters also hate extremes. They can't stand too much heat or cold; they dislike draughts and loathe dampness. An ordinary room temperature, comfortable for human beings, suits them admirably.

* * *

A room cage will keep your pet happy and also give you a better chance to watch him easily. Minimum measurements should be 20 by 10 by 12 inches. Like all rodents, hamsters are great gnawers. A metal cage can take care of this propensity, but if the cage is made of wood, it should be a hardwood, smooth, and at least $5/8$-inch thick. The front can be of wire mesh, or glass or clear plastic, well ventilated. Hamsters are inquisitive, ever busy little animals, and they should be given something in the cage that will help to keep them occupied. A treadwheel is always a favourite. Ladders and tiny slides are also popular toys. Give them a small log of wood to gnaw. This will keep them from destroying their wooden home!

The bottom of the cage should be removable—a tin tray or piece of well-fitting asbestos or plastic—for cleaning. Feeding dishes and water troughs should be heavy-based. Hamsters tend to shift the furniture of their homes and are liable to flood the floor or scatter food around the place while doing it. They are extremely clean and hygienic animals, and if you place a toilet tray (or a jam jar lying on its side with sand in it) they will soon learn to use the same corner each time.

Hamsters also like to make their own beds. You provide the material and they will do the rest. Let them have some hay, bits of cotton, the stuffing from an old cushion or pillow, or bits of torn newspaper, and they will soon make themselves comfortable. There is no need to provide separate sleeping quarters.

Feeding

Hamsters will eat almost anything. One meal a day is usually enough. You will have to determine the amount to give by experiment, but remember that you cannot overfeed a hamster. Once he has eaten enough he will stuff his cheek pouches with what is left over and store it assiduously in some corner of his cage, covering it with whatever material is to hand to hide it. This can be a useful habit from the hamster's point of view, especially with an absent-minded owner who forgets to feed his pet occasionally—although this is most emphatically not recommended. On the other hand, if you have to go away for the weekend, you can be happy to know that your pet won't starve—he'll merely dig into some of his secret store.

Start your hamster off with about 2 tablespoons of food a day. If that seems too much gradually cut it down, but don't give him less than 1 tablespoon. Plenty of fresh drinking water should always be available. Hamsters are nocturnal creatures in the wild, so an evening meal generally suits them best. There are perfectly adequate proprietary mixtures made up for hamster feeding sold in most pet shops. Table-scraps, cheese, cereals, root vegetables, egg, cooked meat and fish, weeds such as clover, plantain, and dandelion, acorns, peanuts, and chestnuts are all acceptable to the omnivorous hamster. A tablespoon of sweetened milk will always be appreciated. But onions, garlic, swedes, raw carrots, and beetroot are not recommended. Stale bread and hard biscuits will help your pet to gnaw, but your finger can be mistaken for a biscuit, and get bitten. Hamsters are notoriously short-sighted!

Remove any stale and decaying food from the floor regularly, but don't visit the hamster's store cupboard too often. He may get upset and try to store all his food permanently in his cheeks. This will eventually cause ulcers and abscesses.

Health
With good care and housing, hamsters remain remarkably healthy throughout their rather brief lives. Skin diseases are virtually their only trouble. If sores appear on their noses and in their ears consult your vet. He should be able to provide the necessary cure. He should also be consulted about abscesses in the cheek pouches. These are more difficult to treat. Mange sometimes attacks a hamster's

coat. This should not be confused with moulting, which takes place seasonally, and is perfectly natural.

Occasionally a hamster may succumb to excessive cold. You may find him lying stretched out, stiff and apparently lifeless. Lay him on a warm, covered hot-water bottle and massage his body gently. Many an apparently frozen hamster has been fully restored by this method.

Breeding

A *doe* is sexually mature at 5 weeks of age, but the best age for mating is around 4 months. The *stag* should be a little older. The doe comes into season every 4 or 5 days. Handle the mating pair with gloves. The doe must be in the mood to accept the stag. If she isn't, and in fact, immediately after a successful mating, she will attack her husband, and it won't be for fun. Hence the gloves. A doe's breeding season ends after a maximum of 12 months. but a stag is good for service for 2 years. A hamster's life expectancy is only about 3 years.

The period of gestation is surprisingly short. The babies are born after about 16 days, blind, deaf, and naked. The litter may consist of anything from 1 to 17 *kittens*, as the young are called. Any sickly or dead kittens are eaten up by the mother. She has an unerring instinct in this matter, so do not be distressed.

After about 12 days the kittens will start to crawl out of the nest. Don't frighten or disturb the mother too much at this stage. She may panic and put her young in her cheek pouches, where they can easily suffocate. After 14 days they will be crawling about the cage, nibbling at some of the solid food. After 3 weeks they are able to look after themselves and should be removed from their mother. At 6 weeks the sexes should be separated in order to circumvent the ever-present danger of fighting. This is the time to get rid of unwanted hamsters. If you allow the litters to interbreed you will soon run out of cages, and very quickly have to move house.

Kinds of hamsters

Varieties of golden hamster are still being developed. Shades such as normal, golden fawn, golden agouti, pied, cream, and pure white are exhibited at shows. The many clubs and societies formed for breeding these delightful creatures are the best source of information for the novice who intends to breed for exhibition.

Cavies (guinea pigs)

Domestic cavies are descended from the wild cavies of South America. They were kept by the Incas of Peru as pets and for food. 200 years ago the Dutch are believed to have brought some pairs to Europe from their South American colony of Guiana. This explains the "guinea" part of their popular name, *guinea-pig*. In those days the animal may have looked more pig-like than it does now. Breeders refer to them all as *cavies*.

Cavies are small hairy animals, about 6—10 inches long. Their coats and colours are varied, and they have no tails. Cavies make ideal pets for children. They are gentle and tame, with no risk of biting. They are cheap to buy, clean in their habits, and easy to feed. They are also remarkably healthy. Their hardiness has, regrettably, led to their wide use for medical experiments, and in this capacity the word "guinea-pig" has taken on added meaning as one who is experimented with.

Buying
Most pet shops stock cavies, and the common varieties should only cost you a few shillings. Generally speaking, the larger the animal, the healthier it is likely to be. Eyes should be bright, and the whole manner should be alert, but some animals are more timid than others purely because they have not been handled frequently.

Housing
Cavies are extremely friendly and gregarious animals. They also breed prolifically. Hutches such as those built for rabbits are ideal. In these the animals may be kept singly, in pairs, in small groups, or in colonies. The hutch should have sleeping quarters and a run. The more space a cavy has for exercise, the happier he will be. Cavies can also be lodged with other non-aggressive animals, such as rabbits or poultry, if that is convenient. The hutch should have a minimum of 3 square feet of floor space per animal. Its minimum height should be 18 inches.

The entrance should be large enough to allow access for

feeding and cleaning. Sawdust to a minimum depth of 1 ½ inches should be laid on the floor, with a covering of hay over that. The hutch should be cleaned out at least once a week, but more often, of course, if there is obviously soiled or wet hay lying about. All stale or fouled food and water should be removed regularly. The wire mesh to the hutch must be small enough to keep out rats and other predators that may try to steal the food and attack your pets. Cavies don't mind the cold but they soon succumb to damp. In good weather put your cavies outdoors on the lawn, if possible. A portable hutch (a wire run with some waterproof material over part of it) will allow you to move the animals from place to place on the lawn and nibble fresh bits of grassy floor. If the sun is strong they should have part of the hutch shaded, to which they can retire at will.

Feeding

Fortunately, cavies are cheap to feed and will eat almost anything. A rabbit's diet suits them perfectly. Specifically, greenfoods, fresh hay, carrots, and various weeds such as dandelion, groundsel, chickweed, and clover are admirable. But the basis of their food should be a nightly helping of bran mash made of bread scraps, cereal, and 50 per cent bran. After mixing with water, the mash should not be too moist. Remove uneaten, stale food after each meal and make sure that there is always plenty of clean drinking water available.

Handling

Cavies are not too small to handle easily, and are quite

safe even for a small child to handle. They will not nip unless extremely provoked by ill-treatment. But unless they are accustomed to being handled from babyhood they can be squirmy and difficult to hold. Once they have escaped into a garden the problem of recapturing them becomes acute. The correct way to lift a cavy is to place one hand on its shoulders and the other under its tummy to take the weight. Make sure that you don't hurt it by digging your fingers into its body.

Health

Cavies, in general, are healthy and hardy. When cavies are obviously ailing it is usually because of bad feeding or housing. Unfortunately, there is not much you can do to help them if they are diseased. Plenty of warmth and a diet of tempting food will generally help to start your pet on the road to recovery. Scratches, wounds, and abrasions, if minor, can be treated with veterinary ointment. Abscesses and serious wounds should be seen to by a vet. Constipation is generally caused by a lack of greenstuffs. Lice and fleas can be cleared with insecticide, provided it does not contain DDT.

Breeding

The gestation period in cavies is long—between 9 and 10 weeks. But when they are born the young are practically miniature replicas of their parents. This, of course, is one of their great attractions. At birth, the babies are furry, have open eyes, and have already lost their milk teeth. Within a few hours they are running about with their mother, and by the second day are already nibbling cereals. They are weaned after 2 weeks, and after a further week the mother loses all interest in them and they have to fend for themselves.

You should let the young cavies run with their mother for about 6 weeks, but after that time the sexes should be separated. The females are called *sows* and the males *boars*. The sow can mate within a day of giving birth to her last litter. She comes into season about every 15 days from her 5th or 6th month. She has about 5 or 6 years of fertility and can safely bear 2 or 3 litters a year. The sizes of litters vary from 2 or 3 babies to 6 or 7.

Sows will live peacefully together, as will one boar with his harem of sows. But adult boars should be separated.

Kinds of cavies

Cavies are classified according to their coats. There are three main types: the *English* or *smooth;* the *Abyssinian,* which has a harsh, wiry coat arranged in whorls; and the *Peruvian,* whose incredibly long, silky hair almost disguises one end of the animal from the other. There are many varieties of colour within these groups. Self-coloured cavies, such as blacks, whites, lilacs, chocolates, beiges, creams, and reds, are popular. Other varieties are the *agoutis* (banded), brindles, cinnamons, *Himalayans* (with a colour pattern like that of a Siamese cat), tortoiseshells, tortoiseshell and whites, and *Dutch* (with markings to match those of the Dutch rabbit).

The Peruvian cavy is not recommended as a pet for the beginner because it requires daily grooming to keep its long, silky flowing hair from becoming matted and soiled. It is also more delicate than the other breeds and needs to be kept in a building throughout the winter. Hutch hygiene should be even more scrupulously observed with the Peruvian.

The Abyssinian cavy has longer, harsher hair than the smooth-coated breeds, and this hair is arranged in whorls or rosettes on various parts of its body. There should be at least eight of these rosettes on a good specimen. There are a number of colour varieties in this breed, and the animals are noted for their good temper.

If you want to see any or all of these breeds at their best you should visit a cavy show, of which there are many in most towns. You will then be able to select the breed you prefer and, if you like, specialize in that breed. There will be no lack of help and advice from the organizers of these shows.

Chinchillas

Chinchillas are small rodents that came originally from the Andes of South America. Their bluish, slate-grey fur has been much in demand for many years. In the early 1900s the chinchilla almost became extinct through over-trapping, but in the 1920s an American managed to export a few pairs to California. He bred from these, and soon there were large fur ranches springing up all over North America, and later in Europe. A single pelt can fetch as much as £20, but this book is concerned only with chinchillas as pets.

Chinchillas have bushy, squirrel-like tails, and grow to about half the size of a rabbit. They are clean, have no smell, are gentle, playful, vegetarian, and nocturnal.

Buying
Because prime specimens are highly valued by fur breeders your best chance of securing an animal at a reasonable price is to look for a breeder's "throw-out". The reason for its rejection need not be a question of disease. It is more likely to be for an unwanted mark on its pelt that would ruin it as a commercial proposition. But it could make a very good pet. Even so, such an animal can still cost you a few pounds.

Housing
Cheap, hygienic, functional cages are mass-produced for chinchilla breeders. For obvious reasons, they provide a minimum of space for the creature, and you may wish to let it have more room to play in. In that case, a rabbit hutch will be more suitable.

Feeding
Their diet in the wild is much the same as that of cavies, but scientifically blended food pellets are available for breeding stock. You can be sure that these will provide

all that a chinchilla needs for healthy growth. Fresh hay and some greenstuff are the only other food requirements. Make sure that there is plenty of fresh drinking water.

Chinchillas are unique in that they are the only rodents that require a daily dust bath. This bath keeps their beautiful glossy coats up to standard. The bath can be provided in a shallow tin or a tray, and should consist of fine dry sand, or fuller's earth.

Health

As long as the cage or hutch is kept scrupulously clean, and draughts and damp are excluded, chinchillas remain remarkably healthy. Regrettably, breeding stock are killed for their pelts as soon as they become adult, but there is no reason why a pet should not live for 12 or 15 years. Apart from superficial injuries caused by fights with others of their kind, chinchillas can suffer from colds, constipation, and diarrhoea.

In the case of a cold, isolate your pet if he is one of a pair. Make sure he is kept warm and draught-proof, with plenty to drink. A few special tit-bits, such as raisins or sunflower seeds might tempt him to regain his appetite. Both the other conditions are nutritional problems. Constipation is usually caused by lack of roughage in the food. Increase the amount of greenstuffs and make sure that your pet is drinking plenty of liquid. Diarrhoea is often cleared up by offering the animal a small piece of burnt toast. If the condition persists, you must consult a vet. It may be a symptom of something more serious.

Hamster
Guinea Pig
Lop Eared
Dutch
English
Angora
Mice
Rat

Mice, rats, voles and gerbils

The domesticated mouse is descended from the House Mouse. By means of selective breeding of different colour strains of the House Mouse a variety of coloured *Fancy Mice* has been evolved. The mouse is generally 3 to 4 inches long, with a tail slightly shorter, giving it an overall length—nose to tail—of about 6 to 7 inches.

The different varieties of mice are separated into 4 main groups, according to colour and markings. The first group contains all the mice of a single colour. These are known as *selfs*.

The second group is made up of mice of the same colours as the first group but with tan belly colours. Mice belonging to this group are known as *tans*.

The third group is of mice with markings on their coats, such as dots and splashes. This is known as the *marked* group. Finally, the fourth group is for any type not included in the other sections. These include *Agouti, Chinchilla, Sable,* etc. This group is known as *A.O.V.* (any other varieties).

Buying

When buying a mouse, especially for exhibition purposes, points to look for are a long body; a long and not too pointed head; large clear eyes and large tulip-shaped ears carried upright and not too close together.

The coat should short, smooth, and glossy.

Feeding

Like rats, mice in their wild state will eat virtually anything. But fancy mice, due to their way of life, require a more select diet.

The staple food of a pet mouse is oats and moist bread. The best oats are usually clipped ones, though youngsters, when first leaving the nest, are better fed on crushed oats.

Because of their small size, mice are unable to go long periods without food. For this reason they should be given enough food to keep them going for 24 hours. A teaspoonful of clipped oats plus a small piece of 2 to 3-day-old bread slightly moistened in water should sustain an adult mouse for this period. Apart from this, the mouse should always have an abundance of sweet meadow hay to chew.

Green food may be given sparingly during the spring and summer months. Mice will eat such things as fresh young grass, chickweed, and dandelion leaves.

If the mice are eating a lot of moist food, extra water is not necessary. Mice have a habit of fouling water very quickly, so whenever possible, provide fresh water.

Handling
Mice should be handled gently and with great care. Careless handling can frighten the mouse and cause it to bite, or it can damage the animal. The correct way to pick up a mouse is to take it by the middle part of the tail between thumb and forefinger and to lift it on to the palm of the other hand.

Housing
When buying a cage to accommodate mice it should be remembered that mice are active creatures, and will benefit from plenty of exercise. Therefore, the cage should be as large as you can afford.

The cage should not be too cluttered up with gadgets for the mice to play on. Ideally it should contain a few small branches and ladders, and possibly a treadmill.

The most popular type of cage is usually about 18 by 9 by 12 inches, with a glass front. The top of the cage is perforated for ventilation, and the glass front can be slid out for cleaning purposes.

The floor of the cage should be covered with clean sawdust or peat moss litter, while the sleeping quarters—high up in the back of the cage—should be filled with hay and paper wool. This the mice will shred up, making it softer and more comfortable. The floor covering and bedding must be changed frequently, if smells are to be avoided and the mice are to be kept healthy.

Breeding

Mice are ready to breed at about 10 to 12 weeks for *bucks*, and 12 to 14 weeks for *does*. They are capable of having 6 to 7 litters a year — each litter averaging 8 to 9 babies.

If you intend to breed mice, you should buy or make a separate breeding box. This should be about 14 by 9 by 6 inches, capable of housing a buck and two does, or a doe and her litter. Inside the box, a partition should go across the width to a height of about $3\frac{1}{2}$ inches to provide a nesting place. The box should have a lid with ventilation holes, and there should be ventilation holes in each end piece.

To start breeding on a small, controlled, scale a buck and two does should be placed in the breeding box. When the does are obviously *in kindle* (pregnant) the buck should be removed.

The gestation period is from 13 to 21 days. When the litters are born, the nest should be left undisturbed for 3 days, after which any dead or sickly young can be disposed of. Often, a litter is purposely reduced in order to produce stronger specimens.

The scope for breeding different strains and varieties of mice is unlimited, and top prizes in exhibitions run to gold cups valued at as much as £150. Anyone wishing to breed of mice seriously should join the National Mouse Club.

Health

Although mice are normally very healthy creatures they are susceptible to damp. A mouse doesn't mind the cold as long as it has sufficient bedding for its nest, but damp is a killer. Whenever a cage is washed out, it is important to dry it thoroughly before returning the occupants to it. If a mouse falls ill, it should be destroyed, unless it happens to be a rare specimen. The best form of treatment for a sick mouse is warmth. This will do far more good than any medicine. Placing the cage in an airing cupboard or near a radiator or fire will provide the required heat.

If the mouse is constipated or has diarrhoea a pinch of Epsom salts in its drinking water should cure it by clearing its system. Sick mice should only be fed on warm bread and milk. But any mouse that develops growths on its body is best destroyed, as these are incurable.

A healthy mouse should live for about 3 years.

Rats

The rat is a medium-sized member of the rodent family. This order of animals includes mice, hamsters, squirrels, and other gnawing mammals. Although there are many species of rats, there is only one that is normally domesticated. This is the albino form of our common Brown or Norway rat, the white rat. There are, however, many varieties in colour formed by the selective breeding of albinos with other coloured rats. These coloured rats are known as Fancy Rats and are normally bred for exhibition purposes.

Feeding

Rats in their wild state will eat almost anything, therefore feeding a rat presents few problems. Cereals, such as wheat, oats, and barley mixed with bread and milk will keep a rat in fine condition. Food to gnaw at is important, so such things as nuts, dog biscuits, and carrots should be added to the diet from time to time. A rat will also appreciate a lettuce or cabbage leaf during the spring and summer months.

A small amount of dry food should be available to the rat all the time, while wet foods should only be given at regular intervals. This will prevent decaying food piling up in the cage. Water, of course, should be changed daily.

Housing

The most popular type of cage for rats is the glass-fronted box. This should measure at least 30 by 18 by 18 inches.

The sleeping quarters are usually in one of the top corners at the back of the cage. The rat can gain access to them either by means of a ramp or a ladder.

The floor of the cage should be covered with sawdust, because it is absorbent and easily removed and replaced. The glass front of this type of cage may be removed for cleaning purposes. The sleeping quarters should contain some form of bedding, such as straw, with which the rat can make a nest.

To provide adequate exercise, the cage should also contain branches on which the rat may climb, and a suitably sized treadmill.

Handling
Rats should be handled with great care. The correct way to pick up a rat is by gently closing your fingers round its body and lifting it slowly. Sudden movements are likely to cause the rat to bite, but if the animal is kept calm it can be handled freely. Rats should not be lifted by the tail.

You should handle domesticated rats as often as possible, because this keeps them confident and tame.

Breeding
Rats are prolific breeders. They reach sexual maturity at 2 months and are capable of having up to 6 litters a year. However, it is not wise to allow them to mate until they are 6 months old, when they are better developed and

fitter for reproduction. Litters normally contain 5 to 8 rats, although there can be more.

Differentiation between the sexes is not difficult with rats. The sexual organ of the male rat is placed further forward from the vent than that of the female.

For breeding purposes rats may either live together in pairs, or a single buck may be put in with several does.

Does carrying young should be given more nourishing food, such as bread or meal soaked in milk.

The gestation period varies between 20 and 26 days. The young rats at birth are naked and blind. It takes 3 days for their ears to open and between 14 and 17 days for their eyes to open. Young rats should continue to be weaned for some 14 days after they begin to run about.

The litters can be safely be kept together until the rats reach maturity. The bucks and does should then be separated to prevent early breeding.

Rats brought up together will live together without any trouble. However, if another rat from outside is put in with them they may kill it. The method of introducing a new animal is to place the original rats and the new one together in a new cage.

Health
Rats are extremely healthy creatures, rarely suffering

from any form of ailments. The only ones that might be encountered are rough ears and tails. These can be cured by applying a mixture of olive oil and flowers of sulphur to the affected parts. If the rat's coat is rather dull due to diet, a gloss can be obtained be feeding it such things as sunflower seeds or hemp seeds. A rat that is properly fed and looked after should live for about 4 years, *although it cannot breed after 2 years.*

Mongolian gerbils

Gerbils are sandy coloured little rodents with long hind legs, and long hairy tails. Their bodies are about 5 inches long. Detractors call them rat-like but their owners prefer to liken them to squirrels. Their native habitat is the Gobi Desert, in Mongolia.

✳   ✳   ✳

Buying
Gerbils are increasing in popularity because in many ways they are the ideal pet. They are clean and odourless, they don't bite if gently handled, and they are cheap and easy to feed. Many pet shops can supply them to order.

Housing
Gerbils are extremely active creatures and in this lies a large part of their fascination. If you let one escape it will be almost impossible to recapture. You must allow them as much room as you can. A disused attic properly wired off, or failing that, a large open-fronted cupboard would make

a suitable enclosure. These animals should have props such as shelves and perches onto which they can jump. They are also great gnawers and will quickly reduce any object they can get their teeth into to shreds.

Feeding

Gerbils are vegetarians and will eat almost anything in that line. They are extremely fond of lettuce, carrots, sunflower seeds, and maize. But they will be perfectly happy on proprietary packets of specially prepared rabbit food, that you can buy at any pet shop to save yourself labour.

Drinking water should be provided and changed regularly. Incidentally, you cannot overfeed these creatures. What they cannot eat, provided it is non-perishable, they will save until the next time they feel hungry.

Breeding

Gerbils are prolific breeders. They are sociable family animals so there is no need to isolate either of the parents from the rest of the litter, except to stop them mating.

Voles

Voles look rather like short-tailed field mice, but they have blunter heads, short ears, a brownish back, and a cream belly. They live in grassland, rough pasture, and rushes, where they make a complex pattern of runs through the roots. Their sleeping quarters are many-roomed burrows in the earth.

Buying

Voles are difficult to buy in the shops but easy to find in the country. Farm workers and gamekeepers know how and where to trap them. Once acquired, voles make intelligent, playful, and easily tamed pets. They bite only if frightened or hurt.

Housing

The enclosure should have a glass or clear plastic front and/or sides. An old aquarium is ideal. Cover the top with gauze or very fine mesh wire. The floor should be covered with moss, peat, turf, or sand, and some hay introduced for bedding. Voles are extremely active creatures, and will soon make a maze of runs in whatever vegetation is put in the cage.

Feeding

Voles are hungry creatures and always seem to be eating or looking for something to eat. They appreciate most vegetable foods, especially maize, lettuce, oats, barley, acorns, nuts, hips, haws, and various berries. Fresh-cut grass is also liked, and they derive a great deal of their moisture from that type of food. But to be on the safe side, you should always provide a bowl of water as well.

Health

Most voles find cage life congenial. They are safe from owls, hawks, and other predators, and are assured of a regular supply of food. They certainly live longer in captivity than they do in the wild. They are generally hardy and healthy, and the only things that are likely to trouble them are fleas. A good dusting of flea powder (not DDT) will cope with this.

Breeding

Voles, like most small rodents, are prolific breeders. Males become mature at about 6 weeks of age, but females will breed at 3 weeks. The period of gestation is 21 days. A pregnant female should be removed to a separate box and given plenty of hay for bedding. The young can be weaned after a fortnight, and after a further week they should be ready to join the rest of the family in the big cage.

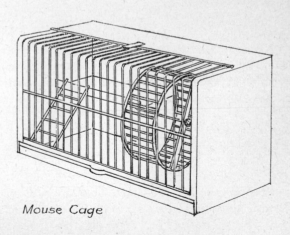

Mouse Cage

Squirrels and dormice

You can take a Grey Squirrel, tame it, and turn it into an acceptable pet, but the odds are against you. Most Greys are unpredictable and some are dangerously vicious. If you decide to go ahead anyway, you will need a permit from the Ministry of Agriculture, because Grey Squirrels are officially classified as pests.

There are no such restrictions on the much less common Red Squirrel which, provided it is caught young enough, makes a truly delightful pet. Red Squirrels are large rodents found in woods in most parts of the temperate world. They are about 15 inches long; this length includes their bushy tail that curls characteristically over their back and is nearly half as long as their body. The coat is bright chestnut in colour, with white streaks on the flanks. Red Squirrels spend nearly all their lives in trees, nervously jumping from branch to branch with incredible sure-footedness. When scared or vexed they chatter shrilly. Captive specimens have a life span of up to 20 years.

Buying

As with so many of the less domesticated animals, the problem is getting a squirrel of the right kind that is young enough to tame. Those generally found in pet shops are imported from continental Europe and are already past the taming age. Tree-fellers and foresters quite often dis-lodge drays containing young squirrels. The babies need hand-rearing, without which they will die. These are your best prospects.

Housing

Because the squirrel leads such an active, extrovert life it must have plenty of room to climb and jump and swing in its new quarters. The usual small animal cage will not do at all. A very large aviary is one possibility, but the best idea is to wire off part of a disused room or attic for its home. It should have nothing less than 10 by 6 by 7 feet high. High in one corner of this you should place a covered sleeping box, about 1 foot square and 1 foot high. Fill this with hay or moss and dried leaves. A squirrel will hibernate under cold conditions.

Within the enclosure you should have branches, a ladder or two, a shelf, and similar props. If you give your pet the freedom of the house (watch your carpets, curtains, and breakable items) his cage can consist merely of sleeping quarters. Ideally he should have the freedom of the garden where growing trees can give him all the exercise he needs. You can do this with a really tame pet. He will return for food and bed regularly.

Feeding
As mentioned in an earlier paragraph, if you get your pet young enough to tame, you will probably have to hand-rear him yourself. Fill one of those little bottles that are used to administer eye-drops with luke-warm milk. Frequent feeds of this for a few days should do the trick. Alternatively, a cat with kittens or a bitch with pups can sometimes be induced to act as foster mother. The baby squirrels should be weaned on pieces of bread soaked in milk.

Adult squirrels are cheap and easy to feed. Apart from an everpresent supply of drinking water they should be fed on nuts, apples, grapes, bananas, lettuce, cherries, bread, raw egg, and cooked potatoes. They will deal with the nuts themselves, of course, but prefer the other foods to be chopped up.

Health
Squirrels are extremely susceptible to cold and damp, but given airy, dry, and reasonably temperate housing they will remain awake and lively throughout the year. Other-

wise they are healthy little creatures, and provided they get a varied diet and sufficient exercise, you should have no need to call the vet.

Breeding
Squirrels rarely breed in captivity. They are evidently inhibited by lack of freedom and privacy. But a young male and female, brought up together in ideal conditions, will mate. The gestation period is 4 or 5 weeks, and litters are made up of 2 or 3 infants. They are born blind and naked. The mother squirrel carries her offspring in her mouth like a cat.

It is a good plan to separate the males before they get too old. They suffer from intense jealousy, and can injure each other severely in their squabbles. But squirrels live amicably with many other pets and you can keep rabbits, tortoises, and cavies in the same enclosure without any trouble.

Other kinds of squirrels

The *Grey Squirrel* has already been mentioned. It differs from the Red in being rather bolder, and being more ready to bite. But it can be tamed if caught young enough. It spends more time on the ground than the Red Squirrel, but is just as active among the tree branches. It will eat practically anything (including raw meat and fungi!) and thrives upon the same diet as prescribed for the Red. Grey Squirrels are active burrowers, so if you do have an outside enclosure, make sure that the wire or netting is sunk at least a foot under the ground.

The *Indian Striped Squirrel* (*Palm Squirrel*) is an attractive little creature, about a foot long. Its underparts are grey-white, while its upper parts are brown with white stripes running the length of its body. It is quite often offered for sale in pet shops, but it may cost you a few pounds, and you will have to offer it indoor heated accommodation, at least until it has become acclimatized. In India, where it comes from, it is one of the tamer wild animals, and seems to have lost much of its fear of man. In addition to the usual squirrel diet, it appreciates insects and mealworms.

The *Malabar Squirrel* is a large, beautiful animal that may reach 3 feet in length. It has a deep chestnut back and yellowish white underparts. Feeding and care should be as for the preceding species.

The best-known ground squirrels are the *Chipmunks* (*Chipping Squirrels*). They are occasionally offered for sale and make amusing and entertaining pets if brought up as youngsters. Older specimens are set in their ways and tend to bite. They are natives of most parts of North America and live in elaborate burrows under ground. They also inhabit hollow logs and holes at the base of trees. They are small animals, about a foot long, brownish grey with dark stripes on their backs.

Chipmunks have the well-known squirrel's habit of storing

their food in a secret larder. They carry the food in large cheek pouches to their burrows. This peculiarity identifies them with hamsters, but they burrow like rabbits, and have voices like birds. They eat the usual seeds, nuts, fruit, and insects in the wild, and in captivity can be treated like the Grey and Red Squirrels. They are notorious for a tremendous thirst, so don't forget the drinking water.

Chipmunks, although nervous little animals grow cheeky and affectionate if properly trained. Their life expectancy in captivity can be as much as 15 years.

American Flying Squirrels make delightful pets. They are about a foot long, and live in wooded areas from Mexico to Canada. They have soft, thick fur, greyish fawn above, becoming paler underneath. Their eyes are large, lustrous, and appealing. But their main peculiarity is a web of skin stretching from their wrists to their ankles, forming a monoplane when their fore limbs are stretched out. They don't actually fly with this but glide or parachute from a higher branch to a lower.

They are gentle and easily tamed, scrupulously clean, odourless, and cheap to feed. Although they hibernate in tree holes in the colder regions, they will remain awake all year at room temperature. They are nocturnal and sleep for most of the daylight hours. Their sleeping quarters should consist of a warm, dry box in a cage about 3 feet square by 4 feet high. Give them the freedom of your room at night and they will repay you with affection and entertainment for 5 or 6 years. Feed them as you would a Red or Grey Squirrel, although they will adapt themselves to almost any diet. They sometimes suffer from skin ailments, but in general they are disease-free.

Dormice

The common dormouse is found wild in most parts of Europe, Asia, and Africa. It lives in hedgerows and on the edges of copses and woods. It is a most attractive little animal, resembling a miniature squirrel. Its fur is fine and silky; it has a large head with prominent black eyes and a pointed nose. Its ears are mouselike. It is a natural gymnast, and when it feeds it sits up on its hind legs and holds its food between its fore paws.

Buying
Dormice are not often seen for sale. Nor is an adult specimen an easy subject for taming and training. Your best plan is to look for a nest (usually ball-shaped, in bushes) and try to collect your own young pet. They soon get used to being handled and make affectionate and amusing pets.

Housing
Dormice are nocturnal. During the day they will lie in a fitful doze, but as soon as twilight approaches they become tiny bundles of energy. The cage, therefore, should be large enough to allow them scope for their activities. The minimum measurements of the box-like cage should

be 3 feet square by 4 feet high. Inside the cage you can partition off a covered corner for a sleeping nest, and provided the cage is protected from predators, you can then leave it outside if you wish. Within the cage you should provide twigs, foliage, and a growing plant or two if possible. Hay, straw, old newspapers, cotton wool, anything soft that can be torn and shredded, will do for the nest. Your pet will make full and entertaining use of any equipment you can provide. He will climb and swing from branches with his semi-prehensile tail—all this after sunset. A word of warning: if you are thinking of picking him up and taking him out into the room, don't pick him up by the tail—the skin is liable to come right off. Provided your pet is properly and housed and looked after, there will be no smell. The only sound he makes, apart from rustling in the foliage, is a faint squeaking.

Feeding

The food bill for a dormouse is negligible. The ordinary weeds and berries that are found in hedges will suit him admirably. These can be supplemented with nuts, seeds, sliced fruit, corn, mealworms, and various insects. Clean drinking water should always be available, for dormice are great drinkers.

Health

Dormice are generally healthy little creatures, and in any case there is not much you can do if they do seem to be ailing, apart from keeping them warm and offering them special titbits to eat. Dormice normally hibernate from late autumn until about the second week in April. Most fatalities occur from their being wakened from this trance-like sleep by well-meaning owners who think they are sick. If they are wakened prematurely they will pine away and succumb in a few weeks. If there is a warm spell in winter they may waken of their own accord for a few hours or even days. In that case it is a good plan to leave a little non-decaying food around so that your pet can help himself to a snack before going back into hibernation. Otherwise leave him severely alone.

In the summer he will eat voraciously and put on so much weight that he will look like a furry ball. All this extra fat is used up during his long winter sleep, and he will emerge in the spring a good deal thinner, and very, very hungry. He will recover his normal girth within a few weeks. The chief drawback to the dormouse as a pet is his relatively brief life span. This is a mere 12 to 18 months at best.

Breeding

Dormice are sociable creatures and should be kept in family groups. They are prolific breeders and come into sexual maturity early in life. The gestation period is 3 weeks, and litters generally number 4 to 8. The babies are born blind and naked. They open their eyes after 18 days, and move out of the nest a day later. The coats of young dormice are greyish and they don't become the adult brown colour until they are about a year old.

RUMINANTS

Deer

There are several types of introduced deer in Britain, but only 3 native species: the *red, fallow,* and *roe*. Deer are ruminants, like cattle, but unlike cattle, they shed their horns or antlers every year. Red deer are the largest. A stag may stand 4 1/2 feet at the shoulder. Fallow deer are a little smaller, and their coats are dappled, with white spots on the backs and sides. Roe deer stand just over 2 feet high. They have very short tails, amd their coats vary from yellowish grey to dark brown.

Buying

Red deer are so large that they soon outgrow their accommodation. They are an impracticable proposition and hard to come by, as are roe deer. But fallow deer are comparatively easy to obtain. Wherever such deer are herded together in a park, a certain weeding-out is usually essential each year, in order to avoid a deer population explosion. This means that about June there will always be a certain number of unwanted fawns available.

Never take a buck. They may make adorable pets when very young, but as soon as they begin to feel sexually active in the *rutting* (mating) season, they will attack you in earnest. These attacks can be extremely dangerous, and some owners have been killed by pets that were believed to be perfectly tame. But a young doe can grow up to be a decorative and devoted pet.

Housing

You will need a paddock, field, or orchard for your pet. Half an acre should suffice. If the enclosure has plenty of trees in it, so much the better. Some form of rudimentary stabling to keep out the weather, with plenty of hay or straw in it for bedding, is essential. In bad weather, especially in winter, deer suffer badly from exposure. Fawns can share their home happily with poultry, rabbits, tortoises, etc. Deer are great jumpers, so fences should be fairly high. An ordinary walled garden is not really suitable unless it has gone to seed and you are no longer interested in maintaining an immaculate lawn and tidy flower beds.

Feeding
In the wild, deer subsist mainly on grass, clover, and the bark of trees. Special treats can include plant leaves, apples, mangolds, potatoes, maize, carrots, turnips, and cabbages. Hand-rearing a fawn can be troublesome. The best solution is to invest in a she-goat and induce her to act as foster mother. Failing that, sweetened cow's milk offered from a bottle with a lamb teat will do nearly as well. Feeding must be regular and frequent, and should continue at longer intervals for at least 10 weeks after the fawn has started to nibble at grass.

Health
Deer are naturally healthy animals, but their life expectancy is shortened in captivity. They are fairly susceptible to cold and damp, and too many animals in a smallish enclosure will encourage tuberculosis. They are sometimes attacked by parasites, particularly tapeworms and liver-flukes. If you suspect their presence you should consult a vet.

Breeding
The only practical way to breed from a pet doe is to let her loose with a park herd, and hope that you will be able to recover her eventually, or to arrange with a zoo for her to be mated with one of their bucks.

MEAT-EATERS

Ferrets, weasels and stoats

Ferrets are probably domesticated varieties of the wild polecat. They have been used for hundreds of years to hunt rabbits and rats. They are flesh-eating mammals about 18 or 19 inches long, including the tail. Most ferrets are albinos, with pink eyes and yellowish-white fur. But some ferrets, the so-called fitch-ferrets, have been crossed with wild polecats, and their fur may be any shade of brown.

Ferrets are lithe, beautiful, lively animals that make attractive pets if handled frequently and gently from an early age. They will rarely bite their owners, but strangers should use great caution. Ferrets' teeth are razor-sharp and they will hang on to anything they get their teeth into like bulldogs.

Buying

Ferrets are generally easy to buy and even if a pet shop does not have one in stock the proprietor will soon acquire one for you. Choose a young ferret, because older animals may not be used to human company and may take some time to tame. A healthy ferret will have a sleek coat and an alert look.

Housing

The ferret hutch should be clean and dry. A wire run about a yard long, 2 feet wide, and 18 inches high made out of ½ inch mesh is ideal. A weather-proof sleeping box should be provided at one end of the run and a supply of hay should be available for bed-making. Ferrets are extremely hygienic creatures, and provided they are well looked after and also properly fed they will not smell and are pleasant to keep.

Feeding

One meal a day is sufficient for adult ferrets, but they do need a meat diet. Pieces of rabbit and chicken, minced meat, mice, eggs, are all acceptable. A dish of bread and milk or perhaps some biscuit meal can be supplied as a titbit now and again. A plentiful supply of fresh water should always be available.

Health

Ferrets are susceptible to the same type of distemper that attacks dogs. Apart from the odd wound caused by fighting or from rat bites, ferrets are generally healthy creatures and fairly long-lived. Many thrive in captivity for 5 years or more.

Breeding

The male ferret is called a *hob* and the female a *jill*. The offspring are called kittens. Small jills make the best pets. If a jill is not mated it will probably shorten her life by some years. A jill and a hob get on well together and may be kept in the same hutch until the kittens are born. At this stage the hob should be moved, because he is likely to eat his sons and daughters. The period of gestation is 42 to 45 days and there are about 6 to 9 in an average litter. Jills will produce 2 litters a year.

A final word of warning: don't let your ferrets escape. You have a certain responsibility to your neighbours' poultry and other livestock. If you intend to keep carnivorous animals such as ferrets, however tame they may be, other animals must be protected.

Weasels

Weasels are wild carnivorous animals that are smaller than ferrets but require the same general treatment. One of the great difficulties is obtaining a weasel that is young enough to tame yet old enough to survive. Gamekeepers and farm workers are likely to come across young specimens now and again. They are sometimes found in wheat and hay ricks. To hand-rear one requires much patience, understanding, and luck. But the rewards are great. When fully tame weasels are playful, graceful, and affectionate.

Weasels are about 11 inches long, including the tail. They lack the black tip on the tail that always distinguishes the stoat. The underparts are white and the rest of the coat is brownish.

In the wild, weasels eat rats, mice, and voles. They are also fond of birds and their eggs when they can get them. They are highly nervous creatures and will often appear to feign death in moments of danger. They roll over with twitching legs, and glazed eyes, and gradually become rigid, with every appearance of death. This happening lasts only a few seconds before the animal scampers off again as lively as ever. It may actually be a type of seizure brought on by extreme fright. One way of minimizing these fits is to provide your pet with a bolthole in his hutch into which he can run whenever he feels threatened.

Stoats

Stoats are closely related to weasels and make equally attractive pets if you are lucky and patient enough to be able to rear them successfully. They are easily distinguished from weasels by the black tip to their tails. They have white bellies and there is also some white on their ears. The rest of their coat is generally chestnut. Stoats are a good deal larger than weasels—ranging up to 18 inches in length—altogether much stronger. Their favourite diet is rabbit, but they will eat anything they can overpower and kill. Some breeders believe that stoats will mate with ferrets, although this has never been proved.

Care, feeding, and housing should be the same as for weasels and ferrets.

Ferret

Weasel

Stoat

Badger

Otter

Mongoose

Badgers, otters and mongooses

Badgers are large wild mammals. They are about 2 feet
long and weigh up to 50 pounds when adult. Like skunks
and otters they are members of the weasel family. They
live in woods and fields in many parts of the world. Like
some other animals mentioned in this book, they cannot be
recommended as ideal pets. However, if they are taken
when very young they can be hand-reared and eventually
become quite tame. They have wide bodies with short
necks and flat heads. Their coat is silver-grey with a
mixture of white, black, and brown hairs. They are

nocturnal animals and live in dens underground. Badgers are extremely strong and courageous beasts, and will fight savagely if cornered or attacked.

Buying

Baby badgers are not normally offered for sale in pet shops, but they are sometimes acquired by accident and can generally be obtained in the country when advertised for.

Housing

You will not usually be able to house a badger with other animals. If he is very young you can get away with a heavy kennel made of inch boards and a roof of corrugated iron. Outside the kennel you should have a small run with a wire surround. But as soon as your pet starts to grow up he will need a larger cage made of concrete. The enclosure must be much larger, too, with strong wire netting concreted into the ground, because the badger is a very powerful digger. Unless these precautions are taken he will soon dig or bite his way out. He should have a large sleeping box filled with straw for bedding.

Feeding

A diet suitable for dogs will also normally suit badgers. Raw meat, dog biscuits soaked in gravy, bones, household scraps (raw or cooked), honey, milk, bread—in fact almost anything that is edible will be appreciated by the badger.

Health

Provided your pet has clean, dry, sleeping quarters he

will remain quite healthy throughout the year. All badgers are subject to fleas but any insecticide will clear these up. Badgers do not hibernate in the strict sense of the word, but will sleep for long periods on cold days in winter. They should live for about 7 years in captivity.

Breeding
Breeding badgers in captivity is quite a rare feat. The gestation period is 7 months, and there is a litter of about 2 or 3 in the spring.

Otters

Otters are fur-bearing, carnivorous animals that live in rivers and on sea shores all over the world except for Australia, Madagascar, the Arctic, and the Antarctic. They are about 4 feet long including the tail, and have large flattened heads, and thick, strong bodies. Their toes are webbed, and their tails are flattened to help them when swimming. Their fur is short, soft and grey interspersed with longer and stiffer brown hairs. A male otter weighs about 18 to 24 lb., while a female is about 4 lb. lighter. Of all land mammals they are probably the world's best swimmers and can stay under water for long periods without coming up for air. Although otters make playful, intelligent, and affectionate pets they require a tremendous amount of space, special facilities, and eat up to 4 pounds of fish a day.

Buying
The younger you can obtain an otter the better. If you

can, you should get a pair. Young pairs are sometimes offered for sale but are quite expensive to buy. It is almost impossible to get them to order in this country because experts are not yet absolutely certain about when they breed.

Housing
You will need water for your otter to swim in. He will also need a dry sleeping shed and some shade. The whole enclosure should be escape-proof. The ideal arrangement is a large pool or pond deep enough for diving, with sloping sides. In the middle of this pond there should be an island with sleeping quarters provided.

Feeding
This can be an expensive item. An otter will thrive on 4 pounds of whiting daily, but strips of raw meat, chicken heads, frogs, rabbits, and eels can supplement this diet.

Breeding
Otters may breed in captivity. The gestation period is 62 days and the litter consists of 2 or 3 babies called *kits*, and are usually born in March or April. They are born blind, and weaned after 6 months.

*   *   *

Health
The only serious diseases that may affect tame otters are pneumonia and distemper. A vet should be consulted as soon as you suspect that anything is wrong. With reasonable care and attention, otters should live up to 10 years in captivity.

Mongooses

Mongooses are carnivorous animals from Africa and Asia
that look rather like overgrown weasels, but are actually
related to the cat. They vary in length from about 12
inches to nearly 40 inches and are about 9 inches high.
They are obtainable commercially but unfortunately the
ones that are available in this country are generally adult
animals.

Mongooses have been domesticated for thousands of years
because of their well known talent for killing rats and
snakes. Kept purely as pets, they can be embarrassingly
affectionate, intelligent, and entertaining. The ones most
frequently offered for sale are the common *Grey Mongoose* of India and the *Spotted* or *Burmese Mongoose*.

Mongooses have grizzled, loose fur growing particularly
thickly near the base of the tail, sharp muzzles, and long
tails.

They are extremely brave and agile and will tackle
the largest snake without hesitation. They become extremely attached to human beings but jealous of other
pets, which is a serious drawback if you already own a
cat or a dog. When tame enough they can be taken for
walks on a lead. They are also extremely inquisitive, and
will soon turn your home upside down if given the run
of it.

A word of warning: you must be prepared to devote a

great deal of time to this pet, because it will literally pine away if it feels starved of affection.

The popular belief that a mongoose is immune to snake poison is false. Its immunity is due to quick reflexes, agility, and its habit of making its hair stand out like a cat when it is angry.

Buying
The younger you can buy a mongoose, the better. It will be much easier to tame and will have learned no bad habits. If you have no alternative but to buy an adult animal, make sure that it has been well treated in the past and that it does not resent human beings.

Housing
In general, housing should be as for ferrets but correspondingly larger. Keep the hutch in a warm, draught-proof place, because these tropical animals suffer severely from cold and damp. Mongooses can be allowed out in a well-fenced garden for exercise, and will soon make playful companions.

Feeding
Contrary to general opinion, mongooses do not live on a diet of snakes: they only fight them. Their diet is made up of small rodents, lizards, birds and their eggs, and insects. In captivity you should provide raw meat in lumps for chewing. Chicken heads, pieces of rabbit with the fur on, and whole dead birds will provide the necessary roughage. Water should always be available; milk and eggs are special treats.

Health

If a mongoose is kept clean, warm, and adequately fed, he will not suffer from any serious disease. But if he does appear to be out of condition you should consult a vet. A small quantity of cod-liver oil given regularly should go some way to making up for any loss of sunshine that the animal may suffer.

Breeding

In the unlikely event of your obtaining a pair of these animals, you may expect a litter of 2 to 4 offspring after a gestation period of about 10 weeks. The young are weaned after some 4 or 5 weeks.

Foxes and hedgehogs

Foxes are related to dogs, and are found in most northern regions of the world. The species found in Britain is the Red Fox, familiar to generations of fox-hunters. They are generally found in wooded country. Foxes weigh up to as much as 30 pounds and have bushy tails that are 12 to 18 inches long. They have a scent gland under their tails which produces the foxy smell followed by the hounds. Foxes are swift runners, good climbers, and excellent diggers.

It should be said right at the start that you will never tame an adult fox. Even a half-grown specimen is generally too old to handle. Young cubs are the only practicable proposition. Older animals yearn for freedom, and never lose their wilder instincts. If frustrated by captivity they will sulk and grow spiteful, or else pine away and die. Fox cubs, properly tamed and trained, make delightful companions. They can be taken for walks on a lead like a dog. But all foxes have certain disadvantages. Their enclosures must be escape-proof, they are extremely highly strung and can turn vicious, and they have an objectionable smell which generally means putting them in an outside enclosure. Some owners take their animals to the vet to have the scent gland removed.

Buying

Many pet shops are able to offer fox cubs for sale at reasonable prices. Make sure your animal is really young, and when picking out a healthy specimen follow the same guidelines as for dogs. A pair will be amusing and entertaining to watch as they play in the sun, but they generally take longer to tame than a single animal.

Housing

Because foxes are such good runners, jumpers, diggers, climbers, and gnawers, housing presents some problems. Generally speaking, the run should be built as for badgers, only less strongly. Unfortunately, foxes are rather dirty in their habits and will use their food dishes as a lavatory. The kennel where the foxes sleep should be dark and amply supplied with straw.

Feeding

Raw meat is the staple diet of a captive fox, although young, hand-reared cubs should first of all be fed on milk, eggs, and cod-liver oil. In addition to the meat, foxes require some roughage, and this can be provided by poultry with the feathers on, unskinned rabbits, and dog meal. Some green grass should be provided, as well as plenty of clean water.

Health

Most diseases that attack dogs will also affect foxes, especially rabies. Constipation is generally caused by cooked food and insufficient roughage. If conditions and diet are right, a fox should live for about 9 or 10 years in captivity.

Breeding

Foxes usually have their litters about the beginning of April, after a gestation period of 51 days. 3 to 5 cubs are born blind, and their eyes open on the 9th day. They are fully weaned after about 5 weeks.

Hedgehogs

Hedgehogs are small spiny mammals that live only in Europe, Asia, and Africa. Adult specimens are about 9 inches long, with stiff spines all over their backs. Their underparts are covered in short fur. They have small ears and long noses, and when they are threatened they roll themselves into prickly brown balls.

Although a hedgehog can never be domesticated like a cat or a dog, it is certainly the easiest of the native wild mammals to tame. It will come to your hand to be fed and may even answer to its name. Hedgehogs are extremely active animals and will always seek their freedom. When young, their spines are soft and they can easily be picked up, but you cannot do this with an adult hedgehog without getting scratched. The best way to collect one of these is to slip a gloved hand underneath him and steady his back with the other. If you want to make him uncurl, put a tasty morsel of food under his nose. This will quickly do the trick. Hedgehogs are nocturnal, and the best time to see them in action is at twilight. They can run fairly quickly and swim well, but their usual gait is a slow, rolling walk. They grunt when searching for food and scream when attacked.

Buying
Young hedgehogs are quite often offered for sale in pet shops and should not cost more than a few shillings each.

Housing
Hedgehogs ideally should be allowed the freedom of a garden. Once a pair have established their territory there, they will be quite happy to live in the garden and seek out most of their own food. But in order to make sure that they do remain, it is as well to provide small quantities of food for them at regular intervals, and always in the same place. An alternative to an entire garden is a hutch for sleeping quarters inside a long wire run like a chicken coop. Bury the foot of the wire well in the ground because

hedgehogs are great diggers. Fresh hay or straw should be provided inside the hutch. Hedgehogs sleep deeply during the coldest months of the year but do not hibernate in the strict sense of the word. During mild spells they wake up with a voracious appetite.

Feeding

Although hedgehogs are insectivorous, they do not feed entirely on insects, but also need meat foods. Chopped raw meat, dog biscuits soaked in gravy, raw eggs, meal worms, honey, fruit, and mice are all acceptable. They are extremely fond of milk, but this should be reserved as a special treat.

Health

Hedgehogs are notorious for the fleas and other parasites that infest their spines, but a good dusting with insecticide should help to keep these down. As the animals settle down in captivity, so the parasites should grow less. Hedgehogs are also susceptible to respiratory diseases, especially if they are living in crowded or damp conditions. They have been known to catch influenza and pneumonia. Sometimes their nails grow too long through lack of exercise and may need trimming. They are not particularly long-lived animals, their average expectancy being about 3 years.

Breeding

Hedgehogs will only normally breed if given the freedom of the garden. They will then probably produce two litters, one in the spring and the other in the autumn. The gestation period is about 5 weeks, and litters contain 3 to 7 babies. They are blind at birth and are weaned after about 7 weeks. Hedgehogs are said to mate for life, but two males kept in captivity with females will fight savagely.

THE MONKEY FAMILY

Monkeys, lemurs and bush babies

Monkeys are the most human of all pets, and therein lies the difficulty. When an owner is parted from his pet monkey, whether through changing circumstances, intractability, or fatal illness, the occasion is usually heartbreaking. The loss is felt much more keenly than in the departure of some more conventional pet, and that is bad enough. There are other drawbacks to keeping monkeys. Apart from the initial cost, which can be considerable, there is the expense of keeping them, probably for many years. Monkeys come from warm climates and need a steady, warm temperature if they are to survive. They are susceptible to many diseases, especially colds and other respiratory ailments, to which they frequently succumb. Consequently, vet's fees are likely to be high. Monkeys are also extremely active, and if they are not to get bored and sulky, their cages must be large and well-equipped.

Although charming as youngsters they tend to sour with age, and you will need every ounce of patience and affection to counteract this tendency.

Having thus listed the disadvantages, it is only fair to state that young monkeys can be irresistable. They are strongly reminiscent of naughty, mischievous children, and react in much the same way. Some of them actually grin with pleasure; their eyes may also fill with tears of hurt or disappointment.

Buying
The larger pet shops will always have a monkey or two for sale. Look around until you find a shop that happens to have the particular breed you want. To help you choose, there is a list of species at the end of this chapter, headed *Kinds of Monkeys*. A female of any species is preferable to a male. It is more likely to remain docile into old age. But most monkeys, male or female, generally react with hostility towards strangers. Look for a youngster that moves well and has an alert expression. Avoid dejected or depressed individuals, however sorry you may feel for them. Monkeys can cost anything from £10 upwards.

Housing

Cages vary with the species of monkey you eventually acquire. Marmosets, for example, are so small that they take up very little space, and can be housed in a cage made of plywood, with wire mesh top and front. Minimum dimensions should be 2 by 2 by 3 feet high. But larger species, such as Capuchins, for example, need an aviary-type cage in order to get their exercise. Most species need room heat, at least, in their cages—60° F. Straw, hay, bits of old blankets or rugs—anything warm will do for bedding. With a tray on the floor, covered with sawdust, your cleaning problems will be reduced to a minimum.

Cold, damp, and draughts can prove fatal to monkeys, but a stuffy, overheated atmosphere will not help them either. Adequate ventilation is essential, and on fine sunny days you should be able to take your pet out into the open. Many owners tie a thin chain round the monkey's waist and take their pet for a walk as they would a dog. If you think that your monkey is not as clean as he should be, sponge him down occasionally with warm water. But do remember to dry him off gently but thoroughly afterwards.

Feeding

Most monkeys appreciate the same type of diet. Where they differ is in quantities. Although they are basically vegetarian, they will depart from this diet to eat minced meat, mealworms, insects, and shredded fish. Otherwise, they should be fed on such fresh vegetables as lettuce, celery, and cucumber. Other basic items of their diet are nuts of all kinds, cooked potatoes and rice, biscuits, chocolate, fresh and dried fruit, sweetened bread, and eggs. Fresh water should always be available, and an occasional saucer of milk is always appreciated. Two meals a day are sufficient.

Health

Coughs and colds leading to serious respiratory illnesses such as tuberculosis and pneumonia are always likely with monkeys, as they try to get acclimatized to a colder climate. Consult your vet if the monkey shows obvious signs of losing weight. But the chief problem is usually boredom, or a feeling of neglect. This is usually manifested in tail-chewing or fur-plucking. A monkey is naturally an extremely active animal, accustomed to swinging through trees and hanging from branches, so give him plenty to play with.

Shelves, swings, trapezes, a ball, an old rubber tyre— all these will help to keep him occupied. Having been deprived of his mother at an early age, he probably feels the lack of affection so keenly that he will either pine away or else master your life completely, and literally hang around your neck every minute of the day. One way to counteract these two extremes is to get him a playmate to share his cage. If you cannot or do not want to invest in another monkey, there are a number of more humdrum pets that will make suitable companions. Dogs, cats, rabbits, guinea-pigs and some birds will live peaceably together with monkeys as companions after a proper introduction.

Kinds of monkeys

Monkeys fall into two distinct groups: the *New World* (Central and South America) monkeys, and the *Old World* (Africa and Asia) monkeys. New World monkeys have widely spaced nostrils and prehensile tails. Most of them are tree-dwellers that are active during the day. Old World monkeys have nostrils close together, and they are the only ones with cheek pouches.

Of the New World monkeys perhaps the *marmosets,* of which there are many different kinds, are the most popular as pets. They are the tiniest New World monkeys. They are less active than most monkeys, and their tempers are generally more reliable. They have wizened faces, ear tufts, and long tails. They are less hardy than other monkeys, but well looked after they should live for about 15 years, and once they have overcome their initial timidity, they make touching, amusing, and confiding pets. They thrive best in pairs and may be induced to breed in captivity. The gestation period is just under 5 months, and 2 babies are normally produced.

Adult marmosets are about 11 inches long, with a tail about a foot long. The Common Marmoset is the variety usually found in pet shops. Its fur is black, banded with grey. Its ears are hidden behind large tufts of white hair. The most beautiful is the Lion Marmoset. Its fur is soft and silky, and bright gold in colour. It forms a mane on the head and neck. Its face and the palms of its hands and soles of its feet have a purple tinge. The White-Eared

Marmoset is similar to the Common Marmoset except that it has black limbs, and its fur is speckled instead of banded with grey.

The highly intelligent, medium-sized *capuchins* also make good pets, because they are usually quite docile. They are about 14 inches long, with long, prehensile tails. Their stout bodies are dark brown with traces of yellow, and a dark band runs over their heads from the nape of the neck to the base of the nose. They are easily tamed and react emotionally with almost human expressions on their faces. Insects, fruits, vegetables, and nuts make up their diet.

Squirrel Monkeys are closely related to capuchins. They are among the smallest of monkeys and are extremely pretty. They are about the same size as marmosets and require the same treatment. They are gentle, cuddly creatures, with soft fur and big bay eyes. Their fur is greyish, tinged with black and gold. They are extremely agile and playful, but less hardy than some. In nature they are largely insectivorous, and will quickly rid your room of any unwanted flies or spiders. Rather similar to the squirrel monkeys are the *titi* or *callithrix monkeys*. They have bushy tails, longer fur, and smaller eyes. They are docile creatures, as agile as the squirrels, but more vocal. The Red Titi has a dark grey back and tail, and tawny underparts. The White-Collared or Widow Titi has reddish black fur. It has a white collar round its face, and a reddish white one round its neck.

Nocturnal douroucoulis, also called *night monkeys* and

owl monkeys, are remarkable little creatures, active at night. They are about the size of squirrel monkeys, with thick fur, white eyebrows, and enormous eyes. They are extremely timid animals that hide away during the day. The Three-Banded Douroucouli is a pretty, grey-brown animal with three black lines on top of its head. If annoyed it strikes out and scratches with its fore feet.

Larger but attractive animals are the *Humbold's woolly monkeys*. They have black faces and are covered with dense, dark fur. Their bodies may be 2 feet long, with tails as long again. They are quiet, gentle monkeys that react well to attention and will settle down happily with your other pets.

Guenons, macaques, mangabeys, and baboons are the Old World monkeys most commonly kept as pets. Of these the most popular are the *guenons*. They form a large tribe of tropical African species that are mainly arboreal. The insects, fruit, and vegetables that they gather are stored in large cheekpouches and carried to their larders. Most species are hardier than their South and Central American counterparts, but they still need some heat in their quarters. When young they are endearing pets, full of mischief, and good mixers. Regrettably, as they grow older they tend to become more uncertain in temperament, but this trait varies with individuals. Fed on eggs, fruits, nuts, vegetables and grain, they can normally look forward to a long life in captivity. A number of varieties can be found in pet shops. Among these are the Mona Monkey, which is about 18 inches long with a 24-inch tail. Its grizzled black and yellow fur, with reddish grey shoulders, and white underparts, give it a striking appearance. It has a black mark across its head, and large, yellowish whiskers.

A well-known guenon is the Green Monkey. It is rather larger than the Mona, with a 28-inch tail. Its fur is tinged with green, and its whiskers are yellowish white. The Green is a highly intelligent and independent monkey that makes an amusing pet when young, but tends to turn surly and moody when adult.

The Lesser White-Nosed Monkey, or Putty-Nosed Monkey is another gentle, active, and hardy guenon, probably the best guenon to keep. It is immediately recognizable by the triangular white spot on its nose, in the middle of a face whose front is otherwise quite black. Its fur is olive-green, splashed with yellow. Its cheeks and underparts are white. The Diana Monkey is a brightly coloured guenon rather like the Mona. It has a pointed white beard, and another white mark on its forehead. Its body fur is black, speckled with white, but its throat and front, and the insides of its legs, are pure white. There is a tawny band running along its back and hindquarters. Its face is black, ornamented by bushy white whiskers. Playful and affectionate when young, it tends to grow morose with age.

Sykes's Monkey is a larger, quieter guenon, that will remain mild and gentle towards human beings, even when adult, but tends to display a vicious streak towards other animals, especially other monkeys. It has bushy whiskers round its black face, and the underparts are white. The upper parts are black, flecked with yellowish grey.

The last of the more common guenons is the Patas, Ginger, or Soldier Monkey. This tallish, slim, attractive monkey is extremely lively, intelligent, and teachable when young, but can become quite unreliable as it grows older. It has long arms and legs, with reddish upper parts and white underparts. Its face, hands, and feet are purplish, but its forehead and nose are marked with black. The thick, long, grey whiskers that decorate each side of its face from ear to chin are a prominent feature of this monkey.

The *macaques* come from northern Africa, parts of Asia, and the East Indies. Like most of the guenons, they tend to sour with age, and are not recommended as your first venture into monkey-keeping. They are greedy feeders and their twice daily dish should ideally be a mixture of beans, peas, boiled rice, carrots, and similar vegetables. On top of this, they may still need in-between snacks. Macaques include the Barbary Ape of North Africa and Gibraltar. They are rather thick-set animals, with shorter limbs than the guenons. They also spend more of their time on the ground. In colour they are greyish or yellowish brown, and they are distinguished by large, bare callosities on their buttocks.

The Rhesus Macaque is not only the best-known macaque, but probably the best-known of all monkeys. It is usually the one doing special tricks at circuses and fairs. It is about 18 inches long, with a tail half as long. Its fur is light brownish, with reddish callosities. It is probably the cheapest of all monkeys to buy.

The Japanese Macaque, or Stump-Tailed Monkey is distinguished by its 2-inch tail. It is an attractive and hardy animal, with a body about 2 feet long. It has very long, dark brown fur and a red face. The Pig-Tailed Macaque has a short, slender tail, but its body is large, thick-set, and powerful. It has a large muzzle, made for biting, and can be dangerous when full-grown.

The Bonnet Macaque gets its name from the hair on its head which is parted down the middle and forms a kind of bonnet. It is a slim monkey with a long, narrow face, and a long tail. It has a pleasant disposition, is easily tamed, and quickly learns new tricks.

Mangabeys are slender monkeys, forming a small tribe in West Africa. They have long limbs and tails, and many of them have white eyelids. Although they are bigger than guenons, they are generally gentler and less vivacious, and make excellent pets.

The White-Collared Mangabey has a reddish brown crown and dark grey fur splashed with white on the nape of its neck, face, chest, and underparts. The Sooty Mangabey has grey underparts and flesh-coloured ears, face, palms, and soles. The rest of its fur is dull black.

Baboons are familiar to all zoo visitors. Their striking,

dog-like appearance is unmistakable. They have long muzzles and short tails. In Africa, where they come from, they live on the ground in troops, generally under the leadership of a powerful old male. They grub for insects, eggs, roots and small animals of all kinds among the rocks and on the outskirts of forests. Although young baboons make amusing and affectionate pets, they become quite unmanageable when adult, and are dangerous because of their extremely powerful jaws and large fangs. If you insist on keeping one, in spite of the warning, the safest is the Guinea Baboon. It is the smallest, and possibly the least quarrelsome. It grows to about $2\frac{1}{2}$ feet in length, with a tail that is $1\frac{1}{2}$ feet long. It has reddish brown fur, but its bare face, palms, and soles are black.

Lemurs

Lemurs are small animals, related to monkeys, that live only in Madagascar and neighbouring islands. A group of animals living in India and Africa are also called lemurs, but these are a different genus. The word *lemur* means "ghost". Its quiet movements, unusual appearance, and strange, wailing cry account for this description. Lemurs are extremely attractive animals, seem to relish captivity, and are gentle and affectionate. Although lively and active, they are not destructive like monkeys, nor do they grow morose with age. In fact, they can be thoroughly recommended.

Buying
Although at one time quite a rarity, lemurs are increasingly

being stocked and sold by pet shops. They are still uncommon and desirable enough to be fairly expensive,
however. Dealers in the rather more exotic pets regularly
advertise them.

Housing
Although they are not completely hardy, lemurs are easy
to house in a reasonably warm temperature, and require
little looking after. Once they become familiar with their
new surroundings and owners they need not be confined
at all, but can be left to roam the house.

Feeding
A varied diet of eggs, milk, green vegetables, insects,
mealworms, fruit, and sweetened bread will adequately
meet their needs.

Health
Lemurs are extremely healthy creatures and should be
long-lived under the aforementioned diet. They may
occasionally suffer from dog or cat bites. Such wounds, if
serious, should be treated by a vet.

Kinds of lemurs

The *Ring-Tailed Lemur* is probably the best-known
variety. It is a beautiful, cat-sized creature with pale-grey
fur, and white face, ears, and underparts. Its long bushy
tail is marked with alternate bands of black and white. It
has a sharp, pointed muzzle, like a fox's, and alert eyes.

The largest of the lemurs is the *Ruffed Lemur*. From nose to tail it is more than 4 feet long. A thick ruff rings its head. It has a white nose, while the rest of its face and head are black. Body colours are extremely variable. In some the shoulders, front, and underparts are black, while the rest of the animal is white. In some others the underparts, face, tail, and feet are black, while the rest of the fur is reddish brown. In behaviour it resembles the Ring-Tailed Lemur, and thrives with the same treatment.

Bush babies

Bush babies, or galagos, are related to lemurs, and are very much in demand as pets. They have an appealing, cuddly, teddy-bear-like appearance and expression, and are so photogenic that they have been widely used in television and films. In spite of their endearing appearance they are not such suitable pets as some people imagine. For one thing, they have sharp teeth and are not at all reticent about using them. For another, they are strictly nocturnal creatures, which means that they are just coming to life as you are retiring for the night.

They are extremely active creatures and cover 10 or 12 feet at a single bound. If you have one loose in a room, you will just have to pack your best china and your most fragile ornaments. The species vary in size from a type a few inches long to the Great Galago, which is as big as a cat. They have very long ears which they can fold out of the way at will. Their extremely large, lustrous eyes are placed close together in a small, pointed face. Their fur is thick and soft, and brownish or yellowish grey in colour, and they have long bushy tails.

Housing

Because the bush baby is such an active animal it would be cruel to house it in a cage where it did not have room to leap and run in reasonable freedom. A disused attic or loft would be ideal, provided it was warm enough. One or two props such as branches and shelves should be placed in the enclosure. In one corner, well up off the floor and as draught-proof as you can make it, should be the animal's sleeping quarters. A box filled with hay or straw will do very well. Try to keep the room temperature at 65° F. or more. When tame enough, and when you have protected the more valuable items of furniture, you can let your pet loose in the living-room of an evening. Its acrobatics are well worth watching.

Feeding

A varied diet of mealworms, such insects as you can provide, soft fruit such as oranges, grapes, and bananas, mealworms, milk, minced meat, and eggs, will keep your pet healthy and happy for at least 9 years. Always have clean water available.

Health

Bush babies are healthy creatures. Cold, damp, and draughts are their worst enemies, and like monkeys they are susceptible to colds that might develop into more serious respiratory complaints.

Rhesus

Monkeys

Capuchin

Spider

Woolly

Marmoset

Vervet

CAGE AND AVIARY BIRDS

Canaries

The canary is a small bird belonging to the finch family. It is a native of the Azores, Madeira, and the Canary Islands—small groups of islands off the west coast of Africa.

The wild canary from which our domestic breeds originated is a small grey-green bird with yellow patches on its body. From this bird, over the centuries, man has bred a number of distinct varieties widely differing in colour and size.

Kinds of canaries

Perhaps the most popular type of canary as a pet is the *Border Fancy*. This bird is the smallest type of the breeds of canaries. Its colours vary, the most common being buff and yellow. Markings on these birds can be either variegated or even. The Border Fancy is a lively and hardy bird, and a very sweet singer, but undoubtedly the best singing canary is the *Roller*. Similar in size and shape to the Border Fancy, these birds are simply living musical-boxes. The melody achieved by this bird cannot be attained by any other variety. Its voice does, however, have to be cultivated in order to bring out its full range and beauty. The Roller Canary, in fact, makes a perfect pet and a very lovable companion, and is just as popular as the Roller.

Norwich and *Yorkshire Canaries*, both plain and crested, can make excellent pets, but as they are more generally kept and bred for exhibition purposes, they tend to be a little more expensive to buy. These birds are normally yellow or buff, but they can, due to a process known as *colour feeding* (*See* section on Colour Feeding, p. 144), be made a deep orange or peach colour.

The Yorkshire Canary is a long slim bird with an erect carriage. It is normally between 6 and 6 ½ inches in length. The Norwich Canary is roughly the same length but because of its girth, which is half as much again as that of the Yorkshire Canary, it appears much shorter and stouter.

White canaries of the more popular varieties are rapidly becoming accepted as pets. With their pure white plumage and sweet singing voices, *White Rollers,* for example, make most enviable pets.

Care and Feeding
Whatever variety you choose, your first consideration must be condition. A healthy bird should have bright eyes and a tight plumage, and should appear lively and interested in its surroundings. A bird that sits on its perch in a listless and droopy manner and has ruffled feathers should be avoided.

A canary is a delicate bird and, when handling it, you must use the utmost care. A bad grip on a bird can easily cause injury, so if in doubt release it and let it settle down before trying again. The safest way to hold a canary is to lay it in the palm of your hand and place your thumb lightly across the back of its neck. This method keeps the bird perfectly secure without having to grip its body. To turn it over, merely take its wing tips and the root of its tail between your thumb and first two fingers and let go of its neck.

From time to time, your canary's beak and claws may require some attention. With very little to wear them down, they become overgrown and will eventually cause your bird some discomfort. The remedy is to trim the beak and claws with a pair of sharp nail scissors. You must take care to avoid damaging the bird during this operation. When cutting its claws make sure that the vein that runs part of the way up each claw is not touched. You can find this vein by holding the bird's foot up to the light, when you will see a red line in each claw. This line is the vein. You should not cut any closer than an $1/8$-inch from the end of it.

If you are in any doubt about cutting the claws or the beak of your bird, take it along to your vet.

The staple diet of your bird should be made up of a 2 to 1 mixture of canary seed and summer rape. This should be varied every other day by the addition of a mixture of linseed, niger, teazle, gold of pleasure, hemp, black rape, or maw seed. These can all be obtained through your pet dealer, or bought ready mixed in packets of canary food. A useful occasional addition to the diet is egg food, again available in your pet shop. Half a teaspoon of egg food given twice a week should be enough.

Green food is an essential to a healthy diet. It should always be given fresh, and free from water and frost. Dandelion is the most popular and beneficial form of green food. The young tender heart and a few green leaves, fed three times a week, is quite sufficient. Practically any green food can be made part of your bird's diet. A few examples are watercress, cabbage, spinach, carrot, chickweed, and plantain stalk. Titbits, fed from the table, should be avoided. Sugar, bread and butter, and similar foods have no part in a canary's diet. Fresh water must, of course, be available at all times. To enable your bird to keep its beak sharp, you can fix a piece of cuttlefish bone in a bracket in its cage. This will also aid its digestion, because a certain amount will be eaten. Always ensure that all food and water vessels are kept scrupulously clean. This will play an important part in protecting the health of your pet. Once a year, you will notice that your canary drops its old feathers and grows new ones. This is a perfectly natural occurrence, known as *moulting*. Each year, any time after mid-July, your canary will start to moult. This will continue for several weeks, during which time the bird will probably stop singing, and look very sorry for itself. Throughout this period, green food should be offered every day, and the seed mixture should be enriched with a little extra linseed. As well as this, egg food mixed with a little maw seed should be given.

You can provide your canary with a bath by filling a shallow bowl with water. During the moult this should be offered about 3 times a week. If your canary does not want to bathe, do not force it.

Colour Feeding

If you have a canary of the Yorkshire or Norwich type you may wish to colour feed it. This process will change a yellow coat to a deep orange, or a buff coat to a peach shade. The colouring food is Spanish sweet red pepper, which is almost tasteless. It should be mixed with the egg food, or bought ready mixed from a pet shop. Colour feeding should start in early July and continue daily throughout the moult—10 to 12 weeks. Give the bird about half a teaspoonful of the mixture a day for the first fortnight, then gradually increase this to a whole teaspoonful a day. Colour feeding will work on any normal coloured types, but only Yorkshire and Norwich canaries are normally colour fed for exhibition.

Cages

There are many types of cages suitable for canaries, but perhaps the most comfortable—from the canary's point of view—is the box cage. This is merely a wooden box with a wire front. Naturally, the larger the cage, the better it is for the canary; a cage of this type with minimum dimensions of 20 by 16 by 11 inches is really quite sufficient. Two perches from the wire front to the back of the cage, and a cross perch running the length to the cage, will leave ample space for your bird to exercise and fly. The whole of the bottom of the cage must be covered with some form of removable sand tray.

Perches should be oval in shape with the flat curve uppermost. Round perches cause cramp, sore feet, broken toenails, and sometimes broken joints.

Although the box cage may not be as pleasing to the eye as other all-metal and ornamental cages on the market, it is undoubtably more comfortable and sheltering for its inmates. When positioning your canary cage make sure it is not exposed to any draughts or to the direct glare of the sun.

Breeding

Breeding canaries is not difficult. They breed reasonably readily—in the right conditions—and throughout, are particularly fascinating to observe. To begin breeding canaries, you must first acquire a breeding cage. This is usually 36 by 16 by 11 inches and is supplied with a means of dividing it into 2 compartments with either a wire or a wooden slide. In each compartment you will require 2 of everything—2 drinkers, 2 feeders, etc. At the back of each compartment, fix a small brass cup hook. These hooks will eventually hold the nest pans. Cover the floor of the cage with gritty sand and a lot of fine oyster-shell grit. Finally, place the wooden partition in its slot. You now have a breeding cage prepared for a pair of birds. When choosing a breeding pair, you should consult your dealer or a fancier. It is not advisable to start breeding with 2 winners direct from the show bench. First, 2 such birds will be very expensive and second, the fact that the birds are both excellent examples does not necessarily mean that their offspring will be of the same standard. For this reason, Border Fancy or Roller Canaries are a wiser choice when making a start at breeding. These birds, often lacking in certain show points, are sold at the end of breeding seasons at greatly reduced prices by fanciers.

Sexing canaries is difficult. For breeding purposes it is often safer to buy a pair from a dealer or a fancier. With their experience they are able to tell a cock from a hen where a novice might find no indication whatsoever. In general, however, the cock tends to have a "bolder" look about him and his head is inclined to be slightly flatter than that of a hen. Cocks are also usually better singers than hens. The best pairing is a yellow bird with a buff bird. The offspring of such matings have better feather texture and colour. Canaries mature at about 12 months, and will breed for several years if kept healthy condition.

Having obtained your breeding pair, place the cock in one side of the cage and the hen in the other. Until this moment, the birds should be kept apart. The time to pair the birds should be about mid-April. As the mating season draws closer, you will be able to see a stepped-up activity on the part of the cock. He will sing noisily and dance about on his perch. Occasionally he will regurgitate his food on the ends of his perch. This is quite normal at this time. The hen, on the other side of the partition, will become impatient and begin to gather anything bearing a resemblance to nesting material. When, after a few days, the birds' excitement increases, and they start calling to each other, remove the wooden slide and put the wire one in its place. Watch the birds carefully. Only remove the wire slide when the cock starts feeding the hen through the partition. The removal of the slide will sometimes result in a fight, usually because the cock makes premature advances. The birds should calm down after a while, when the cock will again start to feed the hen. If they should continue to fight, separate them for a few days before trying again.

When the birds eventually settle down, let them have some egg food mixed with a little maw seed; a teaspoonful every other day should be offered. The hen will now show signs of wanting to build a nest. From your pet dealer you must purchase a nest pan and some nesting material. Hang the nest pan on the hook at the back of the cage and scatter a small amount of nesting material round the cage. More nesting material can be supplied when the hen starts building in earnest.

When the nest is completed, the birds will usually mate. After mating the hen may appear ruffled and dejected; this is no cause for alarm. The hen must be kept warm until her first egg is laid. The first few eggs must be removed and replaced by dummy eggs until the third egg is laid. This ensures that the whole clutch will hatch almost simultaneously.

When the real eggs are put back, the cock must be removed to the other half of the cage. The normal number of eggs in a clutch is from 3 to 5. The hen will, however, generally start to incubate the eggs after the third one is laid. While the hen is incubating, she should not be disturbed. Her diet should be limited to plain canary seed with the occasional pinch of rape. You must withold all green foods, because at this time they can easily cause diarrhoea.

After 13 days, the eggs hatch. You must now provide the mother with egg food as well as her normal seed. The day after the young birds hatch, a little rape and hemp seed can be added to the diet, and fresh egg food given three or four times a day. After a further 4 days, a little green food such as watercress or chickweed may be given. By the 18th day, you may return the cock to the cage. He should start to feed the young. If he doesn't, remove him for a few days before trying again. At about this time, you should place the nest on the cage floor, and if you wish you can put a second nesting pan on the hook. During the season canaries can mate two or sometimes three times. After 21 days, the young of the first clutch will leave the nest. At first the cock will continue helping to feed them, but after about a week they should be capable of feeding themselves.

Exhibiting

If you intend to exhibit canaries, you should join a local canary fanciers' society. Addresses of such societies can be found either in the weekly paper *Fur and Feather*, or by asking your pet dealer. The most popular birds for exhibition purposes are the Yorkshire and Norwich varieties.

Health

Canaries are not subject to many ailments. The most common causes of ill-health are draughts and stale or bad food, or the wrong kind of food. A clean cage will go a long way towards keeping your bird healthy. Minor ailments such as constipation or diarrhoea are easily cured. In each case keep the bird warm. For diarrhoea, cut out all green food and add one of the proprietary bird tonics (available from your pet dealer) to its drinking water. For constipation, cut out hard seed from the diet and reduce the quantity of green food. The best food for this condition is a milk sop. A pinch of Epsom or Glauber salts added to the drinking water will work wonders.

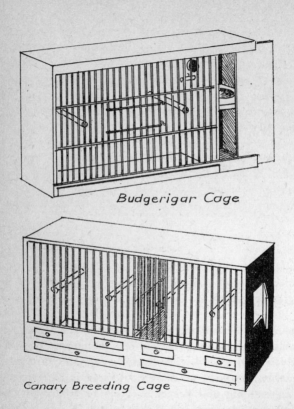

Budgerigar Cage

Canary Breeding Cage

Budgerigars

Budgerigars (or budgies) are also called parrakeets, and are closely related to lovebirds. They belong to the parrot family, and live wild in Australia where they are called *Australian lovebirds* or *grass parrakeets*. Budgies are inexpensive to buy and to keep and this, together with their attractive appearance and ability to talk, has made them one of the most popular pets in the world. With reasonable care, your budgie should give you many years of pleasure and companionship.

Buying

When buying a budgie, certain factors must be considered. Cocks often cost more than hens, because some people consider cocks easier to train. This, however, is not always true. What is important, if you require a trained pet, is to buy one bird only. Birds kept together will merely chirp and play, and will be virtually impossible to train. The colour you choose depends mainly on your personal fancy and the amount of money you wish to spend.

Nearly all shades and variations of blue, green, yellow, white, and grey are available. Colours have nothing to do with intelligence, so don't let that influence your choice. Some colours are comparatively rare, so these will tend to be more expensive than others.

The bird you choose should be lively and alert, and fully plumed, and its feathers should have a natural sheen. Birds with blemishes, swellings, or ragged plumage should be avoided.

Feeding

Feeding your budgie is simple. Its diet is basically seed, grit, green food, fresh water, and cuttlefish bone. Seed, which can be bought at any pet shop, is usually a mixture of canary seed and millet, and is fed to the bird in its seed trough. Millet can also be provided as it grows in nature, on a spray.

Like all seed-eating birds, the budgie grinds its food against grit or sand grains in its gizzard. Your bird should be kept well supplied with this grit, which can be bought at your pet shop.

Cuttlefish bone is important for budgies because it provides them with something on which they can sharpen and grind down their bills. It also provides a supply of calcium, which is necessary for healthy growth and for the production of eggs. Budgies will eat and enjoy green foods in small quantities. The best of these are dandelions, carrot tops, spinach, chickweed, and celery. Green foods should not be given unless they are fresh and clean. Any uneaten greens should be removed before they lose their freshness. Fresh water must be available to your bird at all times, and should be changed every day. To keep a budgie in tip-top condition, a little cod-liver oil can be mixed in with its seed. By adding ten drops of cod-liver oil to each pound of seed, you will provide enough vitamin D to protect your bird against most ailments.

Apart from the normal diet, certain treats can be purchased from your pet shop. These usually consist of canary seed or millet bound together with honey, or a similar digestible sweetener. They come in different shapes and sizes and are sometimes provided with rings or hooks so that they can be attached to the cage. These should not be considered as part of the staple diet, but rather as a supplement. When feeding on seed, budgies have a habit of dropping the empty shells or husks of the seed back into the food cup. This will often give the appearance of a full cup. Don't be fooled by this. Blow away the husks daily and keep the cup topped up with fresh seed.

Grooming

Budgies rarely enjoy bathing in water. They do enjoy light summer rain, or being sprayed with an atomizer, as long as they are able to dry off soon afterwards.

They also enjoy rolling in wet grass, or, failing this, rolling on a wet cabbage leaf in the bottom of the cage. After this, budgies preen themselves and dry off with a natural sheen. From time to time, all birds shed and replace their feathers. This is called *moulting*. Budgerigars do not seem to have any set moulting periods. Some will moult at regular times during the year, while others will merely drop and replace a few feathers from time to time. Moulting is a natural and harmless process. However, should your bird moult heavily there will be an extra drain on its energy and stamina and it will lose weight. At times like these the bird should be well protected from the cold, and supplied with extra vitamin foods such as cod-liver oil, wheat germ oil, and the yolk of hard-boiled egg.

Because the budgerigar's bill and nails are always growing, you should trim them from time to time. The bird trims its own bill on the cuttlefish bone, but its nails have to be clipped. This should be done either by a vet or by someone such as a breeder who has a lot of experience with budgerigars. Most people who keep budgies like to let their birds out of their cages at some time. Provided doors and windows are kept closed, this is quite safe. But you should train the bird to permit you to handle it before giving it the freedom of your living-room. In this way you will have less trouble returning your budgie to its cage.

Talking
Nearly all young budgerigars, especially young males, can be taught to talk. They are excellent mimics, capable of imitating almost any sound that you can make. Teaching a budgie to talk should always be based on mimicry. It should be remembered that words have no meaning to the bird.

Phrases that you wish the bird to learn should be repeated clearly and softly. Any sound that the bird hears you make often enough will be picked up. Usually the first words or phrases your bird learns are the hardest. Once past that stage it will start to repeat most sounds it hears. Some birds may even arrive at the point where they can associate certain people or things with the words they know. For example, a ringing telephone might provoke "Answer the phone". This doesn't mean that the bird understands what the telephone is, but rather that it has been encouraged to say those words whenever the telephone rings.

If you want to teach your bird a long sentence, or perhaps a short rhyme, don't try to teach it in parts. The whole piece should be recited over and over to the bird. If you break it up, the bird will probably learn it all faster but will be very unlikely to say it in the correct order. It must always be remembered that the budgie is merely imitating sounds when it speaks. It cannot lip read. Emphasis of lip movements will only confuse a bird, which will try and imitate your lips with its bill. In the past, some people believed that splitting a bird's tongue would help it to talk. This is a fallacy. Not only is it extremely cruel, but it does not improve the bird's powers of speech in any way whatsoever.

Cages

To enable your pet to keep itself clean and healthy it should be provided with as large a cage as possible. It should be large enough to prevent the feathers of a perching bird from rubbing on the wires of the cage. Inside, the perches should be arranged so that the bird's droppings do not fall into food or water containers, or on to lower perches.

The best cages are made of metal, with wooden perches. Stainless steel or chromium-plated metal cages are the best, but if you choose a painted metal cage, make sure that the paint is hard enough to resist attacks from the budgerigar's bill. The smallest cage for one bird should be at least 12 by 12 by 12 inches. Unless you intend to breed budgies, only one bird should be kept in a cage at a time.

The cage wires should be strong and close together. Budgies will soon find any weakness in a cage and start to work on it. Widely spaced cage wire will usually allow the bird to escape or, worse, damage itself. Cleaning is normally made easier by a sliding tray on the bottom of the cage, on which sand and grit are placed. Sheets of paper surfaced with sand and grit can be used instead.

Food and water containers should be easy to fill. To prevent water, seed, grit, and other débris being pushed out of the cage, a glass or plastic rim, 2 to 3 inches high, should be fixed around the base of the cage.

Wherever possible, a bird cage should be hung on a frame or bracket well out of the reach of other pets—especially cats! Inside the cage there should be at least 3 or 4 perches. These should be made from a hard wood that will stand up to the bird's constant chewing without splintering. Budgies enjoy having mirrors in their cages. A bird in a cage by itself will often be seen talking to its image in the mirror.

When cleaning out the cage you should not only change the flooring, but sterilize the whole cage and everything in it. With a well-designed cage, this does not entail a lot of work. Perches must be scraped clean. Never soak them in water. Water-logged perches can cause rheumatism in a bird's feet. At night, it is customary to cover the cage. This serves two purposes. First, it keeps the bird warm during cold weather. Second, it protects it from disturbing sights and sounds such as television, and allows it to rest. The cover is usually made of cloth, the weight of which depends upon its use. If you are covering the bird from the cold you should use a heavy cover. If the bird just requires quiet and darkness, a lighter cover will do.

Breeding

If you wish to breed budgerigars, it is best to keep them for breeding alone. Tame talking birds rarely make good parents. A healthy pair of birds can produce as many as

40 chicks a year, but this is not good for them and the chicks will not be very healthy or vigorous.

To start breeding, you need a pair of healthy 1-year-old birds. You can tell the cock from the hen by the colour of it *cere*—that is, the hard strip across the top of the bird's bill. Cocks have bright blue ceres, while hens have dark-brown or chocolate-coloured ceres. Don't waste your time trying to breed from sickly or deformed birds. This will only weaken the strain. Selective breeding for colour is a complicated process. For the amateur breeder, it is best to stick to breeding the finest pair or pairs as possible, regardless of colour. Budgerigars of different colours can be successfully mated.

*   *   *

Having chosen a healthy pair, your next step is to acquire a nesting box, which is essential for successful breeding. This should be roughly 9 inches high by about 6 inches wide by 6 inches deep. There should be a circular entrance hole on one side, about an inch from the top of the box, and opposite this there should be ventilation holes. Below the entrance hole you must place a perch to enable the bird to hop in and out.

The front of the box should slide out for cleaning, while inside there should be a movable *concave*. This is a piece of wood that covers the floor of the box, and that is dished to stop the eggs rolling about. The nesting box should be placed high up in the cage containing the pair you wish to breed from.

When the hen begins to lay eggs in the concave, you will notice that she lays about 1 every other day. After laying the first 1 or 2 eggs, she will start to sit on them. She may lay as many as 8 eggs altogether. The time an egg takes to hatch depends on how long it has been under the hen, which means that the eggs will not all hatch at once, but in the order in which they were laid. The normal period of incubation is 18 days.

If the hen lays eight fertile eggs, the nest will eventually contain eight chicks ranging from 2 days to 2 weeks old. This staggering makes the parents' job of bringing up their young a lot easier. Any eggs that are not hatched after 18 or 19 days are probably sterile. They should be dipped for a moment into a bowl of lukewarm water. If the eggs are fertile, this treatment will help the chicks to break out. It is worth noting here that a fertile egg will float but a sterile egg will generally sink. All the time that the hen is sitting on the eggs she is fed by the cock.

When the eggs first hatch, the hen alone feeds the chicks. The cock will only start to help with feeding when the chicks begin to feather. After 28 to 30 days the chicks will leave the nest, and for some time will still be fed by both the cock and hen. When feeding their young, budgerigars should be provided with extras to their diet.

Bread and milk, mashes made from the yolk of hard-boiled egg, grated carrot, and wheat germ are useful both for the parents to feed to their young, and for young birds just beginning to feed themselves.

Ailments

To keep your birds healthy, you must make sure that they are clean and properly fed. Run-down birds are prone to disease. A common ailment among budgerigars is diarrhoea. The droppings are green and watery, and the feathers around the vent become dirty and bedraggled. To cure diarrhoea, stop feeding your bird green foods. Keep it warm, and make sure that its cage is exceptionally clean. There are several patent medicines on sale to relieve this condition.

If your bird is constipated, add a pinch of Epsom salts to its drinking water, and feed it small quantities of greens at regular intervals. This should clear up the condition within a few days. A bird that appears run down and ailing and that does not respond to extra care, is probably infected by some form of parasite. These are usually worms living in the gizzard or intestines. In such cases a vet should be consulted. Parasites also live in a bird's feathers. These are usually lice or mites. There are various powders and sprays available to get rid of these parasites, but cleanliness in the cage is also essential.

If your bird appears to be itching round the base of its tail, and plucks its feathers in that area, it may have a plugged oil duct. You may be able to unplug this yourself with a sharpened matchstick or a darning needle, but if in doubt take the bird to your vet. Birds suffering from tumours or cancers should also be taken to the vet. Some can be cured and incurable cases will be humanely destroyed.

Showbirds

If you would like to exhibit your birds you should join a budgerigar or cage-bird society. You will gain valuable experience from a society's activities. Most classes in budgerigar exhibitions are for birds bred by the exhibitor, which are judged on the Budgerigar Society's Standard for the Ideal Budgerigar. Briefly, the Ideal Budgerigar must be in perfect condition. It must taper smoothly from the nape of the neck to the end of the tail and have a rather deep, gracefully curved breast. The ideal length of a bird is $8 \frac{1}{2}$ inches from the top of the head to the tip of the tail. The wings should measure $3 \frac{3}{4}$ inches and should not be crossed. The head should be large, round, and wide, with the curvature of the skull beginning at the cere, and coming outward and upward. The beak should be set well into the face, and the neck should be short and wide. The tail should be straight with two long feathers. Markings on the face should be clear, deep, and wide. There should be 6 well-defined spots on the throat. The legs should be straight and firm, with 2 front and 2 rear toes. The bird's colour should be clear and evenly shaded. Finally, if you wish to get anywhere in exhibitions, make sure that your bird is trained to remain calm while being judged. Birds that shy into corners or continually hop about will lose points.

Parrots, lovebirds and parrakeets

No bird makes a more interesting and entertaining pet
than a parrot. It is friendly, intelligent, and is an excellent
talker. The two most popular types of parrots kept as pets
are the *Amazon Parrot* and the *African Grey Parrot*. The
Amazon Parrot comes in many different colours. It usually
has a green body with varying colours on its cheeks and
throat. The commonest Amazon Parrot in captivity is the
Blue Front Amazon. This bird is green, with a blue forehead, and bright yellow cheeks and throat. Amazon
Parrots are usually between $13\,^3/_4$ and 15 inches long.

The African Grey Parrot is dull grey in colour with red tail feathers. It is a little larger than the Amazon Parrot, being between 14 and 15 $^1/_2$ inches long.

Besides these, there are many other kinds of parrots. A lot of these are sub-species or types of the Grey and the Amazon. There are, however, a great many different unrelated types, the largest group of these being the *caiques*.

Parrots, like their relatives the cockatoos and macaws, enjoy company. If you keep a parrot, it is not enough merely to feed it and keep its cage clean. It requires a certain amount of friendship and attention, without which it will become morose and lethargic.

Feeding
Parrots may be fed on special parrot-food mixtures available from any pet dealer. These mixtures are made up of buckwheat, sunflower seeds, oats, shelled peanuts, and sometimes a few melon seeds. This mixture provides an ample basic diet, but a little canary seed—also available in pet shops—mixed with it will add a lot of extra food value at very little expense. Besides seed, you should try to feed your bird a certain amount of fruit and green-stuffs. Any fruit in season, as well as lightly boiled root vegetables such as turnips or carrots, can be given. If your bird is used only to eating dry foods, it may take you some time to persuade it to eat any fruit or vegetables. However, if you persevere you will eventually get your bird to accept this new fare. Any fruit or greenstuff left

untouched, or starting to wilt or go soft, should immediately be removed from the cage. If the droppings are wet or slimy, the fruit in the diet should be either reduced, or cut out altogether for a time. Parrots, like other seed-eating birds, require a certain amount of grit. This they store in their stomachs to enable them to grind and break up hard seeds. Grit can be bought in pet shops and should be placed in a container hung on the bars of the cage. A healthy parrot will have tight plumage, and be active in its movements. Over-feeding, and giving scraps from the table are often the cause of ill-health.

Talking

It is not difficult to teach a parrot to talk. Most parrots make very good talkers, although some are better than others. The first step in teaching a parrot to talk is to train it to become used to you. Ideally, it should be tame enough to sit on its owner's hand whenever invited to do so. Although you can teach a bird to talk while it is in its cage, it will respond a lot better if it knows and trusts you. Start off by repeating short phrases clearly and frequently. When feeding it, name the food. An intelligent parrot will soon start to repeat things, and to associate words with different objects.

Cages

Most people who keep parrots keep them as home pets rather than in an aviary. The question of a cage is important. Usually, parrot cages are far too small for their purpose. Birds are pent up all their lives in a space which does not even allow them to flap their wings. A parrot is a large bird, and therefore requires a large cage. If you cannot afford a large cage, you should choose a smaller pet. For the larger species of parrots, such as the African Greys and Amazons, the cage should be at least 20 inches square by 30 inches high. The smaller species can be suitably housed in a cage 18 inches square by 26 inches high. Cages are usually made either of metal with a wooden base, or entirely of metal. The latter type is preferable, because wood tends to rot, and eventually smells. Cages should have removable floors to assist cleaning. These should preferably be made of zinc sheeting, which will not rust.

Some parrot cages are fitted with a grid covering the floor of the cage. This is to prevent the bird walking on the floor. If your cage has such a contraption, remove it and throw it away. Parrots enjoy walking on a flat surface, and such a grid can only lead to accidents such as broken legs or claws. Drinking and feeding vessels should preferably be made of glass or china because they are easy to sterilize and, unlike plastic, they do not smell. Besides food and drinking water, a parrot should be provided with a piece of soft, partly rotted wood on which to chew and exercise its beak. This will also prevent it from nibbling its perch.

A clean cage is important to your bird's health. If possible the cage and fittings should be cleaned out every day, or at least three times a week. After each cleaning, fresh sand should be scattered over the tray on the cage floor. A fine scattering of sand, although sufficient for a budgerigar or canary will not do for a parrot. A deeper covering is required.

Breeding
Breeding of parrots does not have a very great following in this country. This is because cock birds are scarce among the more popular breeds such as Amazons and African Greys. In addition, to attempt to breed in the home would be virtually impossible. If you do wish to breed parrots, you must have a large aviary and be prepared to go to a lot of trouble and expense.

Health
Parrots are generally no more subject to ill-health than any other birds kept in captivity, providing they are cared for and fed correctly. If your bird tends to pluck its feathers, it is quite likely that it is doing this from boredom or lack of bathing facilities. It should be given more attention, as well as plenty of fruit and soft wood to chew on. If it requires a bath, it can be sprinkled with a flower watering can, or a bowl of water can be placed in its cage. Sometimes a parrot will contract a form of catarrh. The symptoms of this are sneezing and a thin discharge from the nostrils. Keep the bird in a warm room and wash its nostrils with warm glycothymoline and water.

If your bird suffers from diarrhoea, add 30 drops of syrup of buckthorn to each ounce of drinking water for the first 12 hours. After this, add 20 drops of fluid magnesia to each ounce of water. Again, keep the bird in a warm room.

A parrot receiving good care and attention will live for 40 years or more, depending on the species. It is one of the few creatures that can become a friend for life.

Lovebirds

Lovebirds are small, short-tailed, extremely active parrots. They are about 5 inches long, brightly coloured, and fairly hardy. Their bills are generally red, and their plumage may be almost any colour of the rainbow, although it is most commonly green, red or yellow.

Buying
Large pet stores generally have a selection of these beautiful birds at moderate prices. The blue varieties are usually more expensive.

Housing
Lovebirds do best in aviaries in which they can fly and show off their gay plumage. Outdoor aviaries will do, except in winter. These birds tend to be quarrelsome, and not more than one male should be enclosed with female birds. An all-male aviary is quite safe.

Feeding
Hemp, sunflower seeds, canary seeds, oats, and apple are part of the basic diet for all lovebirds. Fresh lettuce, greens and millet are also appreciated.

Health
Lovebirds are subject to the diseases that affect parrots as a class. Feather-plucking is sometimes more pronounced than with other birds. This may due to sheer boredom, or it may be a vitamin deficiency that causes the habit. If in doubt, increase the amount of green food and fruit.

Breeding
Many species are prolific breeders. They are best housed as separate pairs in small cages. The nesting box should be about 8 by 5 by 7 inches high. Sprinkle the floor liberally with sawdust, and let the birds have some strips of bark or willow for nesting material. The parents should be limited to two broods in a season, and the chicks should be housed separately from the parents after they leave the nest, in case they get accidentally damaged. Most lovebirds will live in captivity for 15 or more years under suitable conditions.

Kinds of lovebirds

Fisher's Lovebird is the species most often offered for sale. It comes from East Africa and is a prolific breeder. It may be kept in aviary or cage, and is fairly hardy. Most of the plumage is bright green, shading to olive on the back of the head and neck. The cheeks are orange, the bill is red, and the base of the tail is bright blue. Each eye is ringed with white. This lovebird thrives on budgerigar seed, in addition to the usual greens and fruits.

The *Abyssinian Lovebird* is tamer than most, although rather uncommon. It has a red beak, with green plumage overall, although there are black marks on wings and tail. It makes a confiding and attractive pet. The *Masked Lovebird* gets its name from its black head, relieved with white rings round the eyes. Its yellow breast and red beak contrast pleasingly with its general green plumage. It is hardy and a prolific breeder.

Parrakeets

Parrakeet is the name given to a number of small, noisy birds of the parrot family, generally with long tails. They come in many bright colours, and some are remarkably hardy.

Buying
Most dealers that specialize in birds will have a quantity of parrakeets. The best-known member of the family is the *Budgerigar*, on which there is a separate chapter.

Housing
Because these birds are noisy and active, they are best housed in aviaries, although many of them are inclined to be quarrelsome. Some of the larger types, such as the Alexandrine Parrakeet, can be kept singly in a large cage, or else on a T stand, such as that provided for macaws or cockatoos. You must provide suitable twigs or branches, because these birds are great chewers, and will exercise their beaks on parts of the cage if nothing else is provided.

Feeding

The basic diet is the same as that for lovebirds—sunflower seed, hemp, canary seed, oats, and apple. In addition, some nuts and green vegetables will help to keep these birds in tip-top condition.

Health

The ailments that affect all parrot-like birds may attack parrakeets. But some of them are quite hardy and robust. and under suitable conditions will live for 30 or 40 years.

Kinds of parrakeets

Apart from the budgerigar, already dealt with, probably the kind most often offered for sale is the *Alexandrine Parrakeet*. This is the largest of the parrakeets, about the size of a small macaw. It reaches a length of about 21 inches. It comes from India, but soon gets used to colder conditions, and can be housed in an outdoor aviary all the year round, provided it has proper shelter from draughts and damp. It has a heavy, bright red beak, and a long, tapering tail. The overall colour is bright green, but adult males have a sort of black moustache and bands of pink and black on their necks. This parrakeet makes an affectionate, intelligent pet, and will talk readily if trained when young. It breeds easily in captivity. Up to 6 eggs are laid in February, and the chicks are almost full grown before they emerge from the nest.

After the Alexandrine, the *Ringneck Parrakeet* is probably

the most popular. It is a smaller bird, seldom exceeding 16 inches in length when full grown. It is also less sturdy all round, but otherwise closely resembles the larger bird. It has a double ring of pink and black round its neck, and the same kind of long, tapering tail. It needs to be caught and caged while still very young if you want it really tame, but in any case it never becomes such a good talker as the Alexandrine. Care, feeding, and treatment should be as for the Alexandrine.

The *Blossom-Headed Parrakeet* is a most decorative bird, neat and gentler by nature than some of the others. Unfortunately it is also rather less hardy, and does not breed quite so freely. It is a small bird, generally bright green but with a deep purple head. There is the usual black ring round the neck, and each wing is touched with red. These remarks apply to the cock bird only; the female in every case is duller, and has a greyish head. Treatment should be as for the other parrakeets.

There is another kind of parrakeet that has a broad tail, as distinct from the long graduated tail of the varieties already mentioned. Broadtails do not as a rule take kindly to captivity, and cannot be recommended unless caught in the very early stages and trained to be finger tame. Perhaps the most common of the broad-tails is *Bourke's Parrakeet*. It is a small bird, up to 10 inches long, but a veritable riot of colour. The underparts are pink shading to grey; there are touches of blue under the tail; the top of the head and back are brown, and the forehead is bright blue.

Cockatoos and macaws

Cockatoos are probably the most exotic members of the parrot family. They are easily distinguished from parrots by the colourful crests on their heads. There are many different kinds of cockatoos, ranging in length from about 12 inches to 29 inches. Also part of the cockatoo family are the *cockatiels*. These are smaller than cockatoos but no less popular as pets.

Kinds of cockatoos

The two most popular types of cockatoos in captivity are undoubtably the *Rose-Breasted* or *Roseate Cockatoo* and *Leadbeater's Cockatoo*. The Rose-Breasted Cockatoo is about 15 inches long, and has a light pink crest. Its back, wings, and tail are light grey, while its throat, face, and underparts are strawberry pink.

This bird becomes very affectionate and thrives in human company. Unfortunately it is only an average talker and is sometimes prone to give out rather harsh cries. It also enjoys chewing wood, and if given the chance will make short work of any fittings in its cage. However, even with these shortcomings, its affectionate manner and beautiful plumage, and the fact that it will stand any amount of stroking and petting without biting, make it a worthwhile pet.

Leadbeater's Cockatoo is about the same size. It is a strikingly beautiful bird whose plumage really defies description. Its back, wings and tail are snowy white. Its underparts, neck, chin, and face are a delicate pink. On top of all this is the large, full crest, red with white tips and a bright yellow band across the middle. This bird is ideal for the aviary because it is a good breeder. It also makes a reasonable household pet. Unfortunately, like the Rose-Breasted Cockatoo, it does have rather a loud unpleasant voice, but this is surely offset by its unmatched beauty.

Feeding
Cockatoos eat the same foods as other parrots, and no special diet is required. Parrot food as bought from a pet dealer, with the addition of fruit and green foods, is quite sufficient.

Grooming
Most cockatoos, and especially the Rose-Breasted Cockatoo, are fond of rain. If you place one outside in a summer shower, it will show great excitement, and hang upside down with open wings, allowing the rain to run through its feathers.

Talking
Although cockatoos rarely become such accomplished talkers as parrots, you can, by using the same methods as with a parrot, teach them a few words.

Cages
Cockatoos are large birds, and should not be cooped up in small cages. The minimum sizes of cages for most cockatoos, apart from the very much smaller cockatiels, should be 20 inches square by 30 inches high. Because of the cockatoo's habit of chewing wood, cages should be constructed of metal. They should be fitted out for cleaning like a parrot cage. The cockatoo is a very active bird and should not be confined to its cage. Given the occasional freedom of a room, it will prove a far more interesting pet.

Breeding

Cockatoos are easier to breed than parrots, and anyone with a small aviary should have no trouble. A nest box with a small hole in the side, and lined with rotten wood, is all that is required—assuming, of course, that you have a breeding pair. Parrots and cockatoos do not normally make nests. They lay their eggs inside holes in trees. This is what the nesting box must imitate. There are usually two or three eggs, on which the hen sits most of the time. When she leaves the nest to feed, the cock takes her place. Incubation takes about a month. Members of the parrot family live to a great age, and consequently are often slow to breed, so the prospective breeder will often have to exercise a great deal of patience.

Ailments

The ailments that attack cockatoos are dealt with in the parrot section. The remedies are the same for parrots and cockatoos.

Macaws

Macaws are huge, gaudy, long-tailed birds of the parrot family, sometimes attaining a length of three feet or more. They have strong, pointed wings, and stout but immensely powerful arched beaks. They are noisy, squawking birds that can inflict a nasty bite.

Buying

Macaws are available from most pet shops that stock the

larger breeds of birds, but they are expensive to buy. Make sure you get a young bird if you wish it to become tame and confiding.

Housing
Macaws are such large birds that they must have a big aviary in which to exercise their powerful wings. The alternative is to perch them on an open T stand, chained to it by one leg. Many birds get so attached to their particular stand that eventually they will not leave it, and the chain can be dispensed with. If you put a macaw in an aviary, make sure that the netting is extra strong, attached to iron stanchions.

Feeding
Proprietary parrot foods, pre-packed, and sold in most pet shops make a balanced diet for macaws, but you can vary this food with beans, sprouts, fresh fruit, canary seed, and peanuts.

Health
Apart from the usual parrot diseases, macaws may some-times look dejected and off-colour for no apparent reason. Try your bird with some soft food—boiled barley or maize—for a change. In the tropical jungle where macaws come from, they are used to showers of rain. This warm water thoroughly soaks their feathers, after which they will preen themselves. Unless they get wet they seem to lack the stimulus necessary to groom themselves. Gently syringe your bird with tepid water from time to time and watch the transformation.

Kinds of macaws

The kinds most usually offered for sale are the *Blue and Yellow* and the *Red and Blue*.

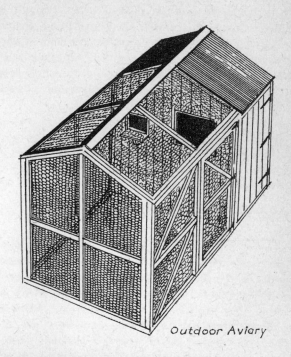

Outdoor Aviary

Crows

The crow family is made up of a number of large, predatory birds including the raven, rook, jackdaw, magpie, jay, and various others. Unless these birds have been cage-reared their sale is prohibited under the Wild Birds Protection Act. But there is no law against taking them from the nest as fledglings and hand-rearing them. In fact, that is the only way you'll be able to come by them, and you'll be doing local farmers and market gardeners and other birds in the vicinity a good turn if you keep your crows under strict control.

Jackdaws

The jackdaw is one of the smallest members of the family, and probably makes the most interesting pet of the lot. It is glossy black all over, and extremely inquisitive. It can be allowed to roam freely in a large garden, once it has been tamed, and will probably follow you round from room to room in the house. It is notorious for picking up small bright objects and hiding them. Keep your jewellery, money, keys, etc., out of sight and out of reach. Like jays and magpies, jackdaws are excellent mimics and can be taught to talk if training is started young enough.

Housing
Jackdaws are fairly sociable, and a pair or more may be kept together in a large aviary without too much trouble. But don't house them with other birds or animals smaller than they are. Like all the crow family, they are great bullies if they think they can get away with it. Weaker creatures will come off badly with them, and may even be killed.

Feeding
All members of the crow family are practically omnivorous. They will eat carrion, however high, and table scraps will be eagerly devoured. A more orthodox diet is dog biscuit soaked in milk or gravy, dried fruits, boiled eggs, chopped meat, greens, and seeds. If you can apportion their diet to one-third vegetables and two-thirds meat you will be on the safe side. Plenty of fresh water should always be available.

Health

Jackdaws are exceedingly hardy and usually quite tough and healthy. Should they be troubled with diarrhoea it generally means that they are eating too much fruit and greens.

Ravens, jays and magpies

Ravens are by far the largest of the group, and because of their size and formidable beaks, do not make suitable pets as adults. If kept at all, they should be put in an aviary, but make sure they have no birds smaller than themselves in with them. They will always appreciate lumps of horse-meat in their diet. If taught young enough they are good mimics of human speech and animal noises. Ravens are alleged to mate for life, and with proper care and attention will live for nearly 100 years.

Jays, on the other hand, make quite charming pets. They are the shortest lived of the crow family, their age-span being about 12 or 13 years. Like jackdaws, they are fond of appropriating bright objects, so guard your loose change. They prefer natural food to specially prepared meals, and for this reason are not quite so easy to rear as the others. Insects and small rodents, with nuts and berries, are their staple diet in the wild. Jays are probably the best talkers of the group, and they develop a mocking kind of tone that sometimes infuriates other animals. Regrettably they are not very sociable birds, and, as they often show signs of jealousy, are best caged by themselves.

Magpies are great thieves and make excellent mimics. Like jays, they prefer to be the centre of attention and like living on their own. They are rather more nervous and jumpy than jackdaws and jays, and for that reason do not make such good pets. With care they may live for 25 years or more.

Mynahs

Mynahs are attractive and accomplished birds, imported as pets from parts of Asia, particularly India. In size they are just a little larger than our blackbirds, although size does vary among the different species. There are generally 4 types of mynah birds available in this country. They are the *Common Mynah*, the *Greater Hill Mynah*, the *Lesser Hill Mynah*, and the *Black-Winged Mynah*.

The most popular types are the Common Mynah and the Greater and Lesser Hill Mynahs. The Black-Winged

Mynah is not imported in such great numbers as the others and is therefore rather rarer. Of the popular types, the Greater and Lesser Hill Mynahs are supposed to be the better talkers and mimics. But a good Common Mynah can often equal these birds in speech and mimicry if encouraged.

Feeding

In their natural habitat, mynahs are fruit-eaters. They also eat all kinds of insects—these are an important part of their diet. When kept in captivity, a mynah should be fed at least 10 meal worms a day. For a staple diet you should feed it a paste made up from a packet mixture available in pet shops. This is specially prepared for mynahs, and includes dried egg and insects. Fresh fruit such as grapes, oranges, bananas, currants, or sultanas should also have a place on the daily menu. About once a week a mixture of boiled rice, and cooked egg may be offered in place of the egg-insect mixture. Fresh water should be made available every day. Mynahs are omnivorous, and will only thrive on a balanced but well varied diet.

Talking

Mynahs are quite possibly the best talkers available. Not only are they very intelligent and pick up words and phrases easily, but their deeper, clearer voices have no trouble in putting the best of parrots to shame. To teach a mynah to talk, begin by repeating a few simple words clearly and frequently to the bird. It will not take long to get the message. Quite soon it will be showing off its new ability. Like parrots, mynahs are able to associate objects with words: for example, when feeding it grapes repeat the word "grapes". Before long it will say that word everytime it recognizes a grape.

Cages

One of the drawbacks of keeping mynahs is the fact that they require so much space. Whenever possible they should be kept in aviaries, which will allow them ample room for exercise. They can, however, be kept as house pets, providing you can find the space for a cage at least 4 feet long by 2½ feet high by 20 inches wide. Inside the cage or aviary, food and water bowls should be kept clear of perches to avoid soiling by droppings. Unfortunately mynahs tend to be rather messy birds because they throw their food about. Also, because of the nature of their diet, their droppings are rather wet. This means that a cage very soon becomes dirty. If you want to keep a mynah, you must be prepared to clean out its cage every day. Before giving a pet mynah the freedom of your sitting-room, protect your furniture and carpets with newspapers.

Mynahs kept in aviaries can often safely be allowed out in the garden. Here they can find their own insects and, if you have any fruit growing, they will look after that part of their diet themselves. If you wish to allow your bird out in this way, the best plan is to release it after mating, when it has young in the nest. It will then go out and forage for food but will not go far from its offspring. This will also lighten your burden as far as feeding is concerned.

Breeding

If you wish to breed mynahs, an aviary is essential. In the breeding season a pair of mynahs will become noticeably more active and start to pay more attention to each other. As both sexes look alike—only an expert can tell the difference—you must buy a pair that has already bred. When the birds are obviously ready to breed, a nesting box and nesting materials should be placed in the aviary.

Other seed-eaters

In addition to the parrots, canaries, budgerigars, and cockatoos, which are covered in separate chapters, there are a host of imported seed-eaters that are variously classified as finches, weavers, waxbills, and others. Many of these birds are small—under 6 inches long, and make excellent, colourful pets.

Buying
Most pet shops carry at least a few of the more common seed-eaters. Others are advertised in the pet journals. Prices vary according to availability.

Housing

Most of these birds do well in an outside aviary, but they need warmth in winter. You must provide covered quarters within the aviary, and alternative nesting sites. Segregate your birds according to size, then there will be less likelihood of bullying.

Feeding

The basic diet is millet, canary seed, hemp, lettuce, seeding grass, chickweed, dandelion, and small insects.

Breeding

These birds breed easily in captivity if they are encouraged by the provision of suitable nesting materials. A box, about 6 inches square, with an opening in the side, should have a supply of feathers, sticks, shavings, hair, roots and similar material. These birds are good mixers and reasonably long-lived.

Kinds of seed-eaters

As already indicated, there is a tremendously wide choice of these birds for the pet-keeper, and the following list is by no means comprehensive, but merely representative of the some of the easier and more rewarding varieties to keep.

Zebra Finches are probably the most popular of the lot. They are easy to keep and breed, are hardy, good mixers, and come in an assortment of colours. They originate in

Australia, and are about 4 inches long. In the male the upper parts are silver-grey, the underparts white, and the tail black and white. The beak is crimson, and there is a black band on the breast below distinctive black and white stripes. On the face there is a black and white eye stripe, and a splash of orange on the cheeks. The female is duller all round. Zebra Finches will thrive under most conditions and require no special care or treatment, apart from those outlined in general for finches.

The *Green Singing Finch* comes from Africa, and is about 4 ½ inches long. It is well-known for its beautiful trilling song, which is rather like that of a skylark. It is a friendly, entertaining little bird that can easily be crossed with the canary. In the male the underparts are yellow, the tail and wings brown, and the upper parts greenish yellow with black markings. The hen is duller with dark dots on the throat. The *Grey Singing Finch* is an even better songster, and in the opinion of many, the best of the imported seed-eaters in this respect. It is a small grey bird that is just as easy and amusing to keep as its predecessor.

The *Cut-Throat* or *Ribbon Finch* also comes from Africa. It is light brown in colour, splashed with white on the throat. The male bird has a band of scarlet across this white patch. Although the Cut-Throat is hardy and easy to breed, it is rather aggressive, and you will have to ensure that its fellow inmates are not smaller or weaker to spare them almost inevitable bullying.

The *Diamond Sparrow* is an Australian finch, about the

size of an ordinary sparrow. It is a beautiful bird, with grey upper parts, crimson rump, and black tail. It has a crimson beak and white under-parts. Across its breast is a band of black, and its flanks are also black, splashed with white. Because of its uncertain temperament with other birds it may have to be kept as a solitary pet in a largish cage. Otherwise, once it is acclimatized it can be pût in an outdoor aviary, with somewhere warm to sleep.

Bengalese are small birds, about 5 inches long, that have been domesticated for hundreds of years in the Far East. Of the imported seed-eaters, they are probably the easiest to rear and look after. They come in a number of different colours, and there is even a crested variety. The male is best distinguished by his curious courtship display when he sings and dances to impress the hen. Bengalese are gentle, unruffled birds, that perhaps do better in a cage than an aviary. They are not fully hardy, and in cold weather in an outdoor aviary will need some heat. Bengalese not only look after their own offspring with great devotion, but also make good foster parents for other birds' eggs. They thrive on the usual seed mixtures and green foods.

Alario Finches are pretty little birds, about 4 ½ inches long. In shape they resemble canaries, and in song they outdo them. The male bird has a brown back, wings, and tail. The under-parts are white, and the head, face, and throat are black. These make gentle, peaceful cage birds, and are quite hardy. They need some green food in addition to the usual seed diet.

A South American variety is the *Saffron Finch*. It needs acclimatizing, but afterwards will mix happily with other birds in an outdoor aviary. Its rather piercing song is heard throughout the summer months. It is a strikingly beautiful bird, with brilliant yellow plumage. It is tinged with orange on its head and green on parts of its back and wings. In addition to seeds, it will eat mealworms and gentles.

Possibly the most sensational-looking of the ornamental finches is the *Gouldian Finch* from Australia. It is only about 4 inches long from head to tail, but has an incomparable blend of colours. There are three established varieties: yellow-headed, black-headed, and red-headed. Apart from the different head colours all three varieties have the same body hues. The wings are bright green, as are the upper parts, except for the rump and neck which are turquoise. The underparts are golden yellow, except for the breast, which is purplish. The hen is paler in all respects, and the young birds are a uniform grey-green.

Gouldians are fairly costly to buy, and rather less hardy than most finches. But provided they get enough steady warmth, and provided also that there is no drastic change in their diet of seeds and green foods, they are no problem to breed, and make tame and confiding pets, as well as being a joy to look at.

A rather similar Australian finch is the *Long-Tailed Grassfinch*. It is between 4 and 5 inches long, and once acclimatized, is perfectly hardy in an outdoor aviary. The whole bird is pale pinkish, with grey head and velvety black tail, chin, throat and upper breast. There are similar black patches on the flanks. The beak and legs are reddish yellow. The two centre feathers of the tail stretch out to almost hair-like points, and it is this peculiarity that gives the bird its name.

ORNAMENTAL AND GAME BIRDS

Pigeons and doves

Pigeons are birds that belong to the dove family. There is no scientific distinction between the two names, but the larger birds are usually called *pigeons*, and the smaller ones *doves*. There are more than 200 species of pigeons and they are found in almost every part of the world. Domestic pigeons have been kept for thousands of years; today there are more than 150 breeds, and many of these breeds contain a number of strains. All domestic pigeons are believed to have descended from the wild *rock dove*.

Domestic pigeons have been kept for various purposes through the ages. *Homing pigeons* have an uncanny knack of finding their way home over long distances. They are used for racing and for carrying messages. Other breeds have delicate flesh and are reared for food. Still others are bred strictly for decorative and show purposes. Some of these have been so closely bred to produce certain show characteristics that their beaks have become too short to be used in feeding their young, and foster parents have to be provided from among the less fancy varieties. Such non-feeders, as they are called, are found among the *Barbs, Short-Faced Tumblers, Owls,* and others.

Buying

Pigeons as pets are easy and cheap to buy, unless you are looking for some of the rarer and more exotic varieties. A visit to one of the many pigeon shows can be an illuminating experience, and expert fanciers are always ready with their advice. You will discover the breeds that are easiest to rear for your particular purposes.

Housing

Pigeons may be housed in various ways. If you have a large aviary they will thrive there. Another possibility is to put them in a cote, which can rest on the top of a long pole, or be fixed high up against a wall. A third type of enclosure is a pigeon loft. Aviaries should contain loft-type accommodation inside, while outside the flights should be enclosed with wire netting. Allow the birds as much room as possible for exercise—a height of 6 feet and a length of 15 is the minimum. Cotes should face south or south-west, thus allowing the birds to enjoy as much sunshine as possible. The cote should, by its very nature be cat-proof, and also weather-proof. Pigeons can stand almost any amount of cold, but wet and draughty quarters will not be appreciated. There should be two nesting compartments for each pair in the cote, and each compartment should be at least 10 inches square. When you first introduce new birds to the cote you must put some temporary netting over the entrance holes to confine the birds to their new home for two or three weeks. This will give them an opportunity to get used to their new surroundings. When they are eventually free to go in and out as they please they will regard the cote as their proper home and return to it after local flights. Without this precaution they would immediately try to fly back to their former home, and probably get lost in the process. Cover the floor with sand or sawdust, and see that the cote is regularly cleaned out. A cote against a wall should be constructed on the same principles.

*　　*　　*

A pigeon loft should also face the sun and give protection from rain and cold winds. It should have a landing platform jutting out underneath the eaves, just in front of the entrances. Inside, there should be shelves and perches. The concrete floor should be covered with sawdust or sand, or some similar material, and regularly and frequently cleaned out. Twigs, bits of straw, hay, and rags should be made available for nesting material. The floors of the nesting boxes should be covered with a thick layer of sawdust.

Feeding

Regular feeding is essential. You may give either one or two meals a day, but stick to the routine. Excellent packets of pigeon food are cheaply available, and will provide an adequate balanced diet consisting of maize, tares, tick beans, maple peas, and other seeds. Pigeons also need grit, a lump of rock salt, and, if they are not at liberty, a supply of greenstuff such as lettuces and cabbage. Let them have two lots of water—one in a flat wide vessel for bathing in (an exercise they love), and another with a narrower top for drinking.

Health

Lack of exercise may make pigeons fat and lazy. They may suffer injuries from prowling cats or rats, or one of their own kind. Their plumage sometimes becomes infested with red mites, but the vet will give you a disinfectant to put in their bathing water that will quickly clear those. Kept under good conditions, pigeons are remarkably healthy birds and have been known to live for 20 years or more.

Breeding

Most pigeons breed freely. The traditional mating day is St Valentine's Day, in the middle of February. You need twice as many nesting-boxes as there are females. Once a pair have mated they will usually stay together until the eggs hatch, always using the same nest. The cock and hen will incubate the two eggs in turn, he by day and she by night. The *squabs*, as the young are called, are born blind, naked, and helpless, after an incubation period of 18 days.

The parent birds regurgitate partly digested food, called "pigeon's milk", from their crops directly into their babies' mouths. After about 4 weeks, the squabs leave the nest, and although still being fed by their parents, will start picking up bits of food for themselves. They start to moult at about 9 weeks of age. But by this time the parents should be sitting on another two eggs in the spare nest.

Kinds of pigeons

As indicated earlier, there are many attractive varieties of fancy pigeons to choose from. Your best plan is to visit a show, pick out a few of the types that appeal to you most, and then ask the experts about them. Homers, Tumblers, and Tipplers are three hardy varieties that are beautiful to watch in flight. *Homers or Racing Pigeons* are extremely well-known because so many fanciers use them at week ends to fly competitively. In this exciting sport they are trained not only to fly far and fast, but also to find their way home over strange country. Homers can be very expensive and should be kept in tip-top condition.

Tumblers or *Rolling Pigeons* turn one or more back somersaults in mid-flight. Nobody has yet satisfactorily explained why they indulge in these sensational aerobatics. It may be a defect, or just high spirits. *Tipplers* are pigeons that fly straight up to a good height and then circle in the air for long periods out of sheer love of flying. The longer they stay up before returning to the loft, the better tipplers they are.

Doves

Doves are smaller than pigeons, and in general require the same kind of treatment. But there are a few important exceptions. Doves should be kept in an aviary, rather than a cote. You can mix them quite safely with other birds such as lovebirds, parrakeets, and finches, but not more than one pair should be kept in the same enclosure. They are murderous towards each other, especially the cock birds. They love bathing even more than pigeons do, so plenty of water should be provided for that purpose. The seed should be smaller than that supplied for pigeons. A mixture of wheat, rice, canary seed, and millet will be appreciated. In addition they will need the usual grit and rock salt.

Breeding habits are similar to those of pigeons, but the incubation period is only 16 days, and doves need open boxes to nest in.

The *Barbary Dove* is the domesticated version of the Collared Turtle Dove, and makes a gentle, easy pet to rear. Its plumage is cream and fawn, and it has a black ring round its neck. The *Diamond Dove* is one of the smallest varieties, being only about 4 inches long, with a tail almost as long again. It comes from Australia, and its plumage is slate-grey, with white marks on the wings. The *Java Dove* is a pure white form of the Barbary, with the same bright red legs and feet. The *Harlequin* or *Cape Dove* is a 9-inch specimen, of which more than half is tail. Although it makes a colourful and delightful pet, it is not as hardy as some, and is difficult to breed in captivity. The hen is brownish, but the cock is marked with black on head, face, and throat. There is a white area surrounding the black, and there is white on breast and legs. The rest of the body is grey-blue.

Bantams, peafowl, pheasants and quail

Bantams are poultry in miniature, and most of the large, well-known breeds have a bantam variety. They are tame and decorative, they take up far less space than conventional poultry, and their eggs, though small, are extremely tasty.

Buying
Many pet shops do not stock bantams, but livestock and poultry papers carry advertisements with bantams for sale, and they can usually be bought quite cheaply.

Housing

Most bantams are hardy, and an ordinary poultry pen or run will suit them admirably. They need a shed of sorts in which to shelter at night and gain some protection from bad weather. A few specimens may be given the run of the garden, provided it is escape-proof. Clip the flight feathers of one wing only and your birds will not attempt to fly away. Bantams will roost in low trees and shrubs. Cover the floor of their shelter to a depth of several inches with straw, hay, or peat.

Feeding

Bantams eat the same as ordinary domestic poultry. Give them an evening meal each day of whole grain, preferably wheat or a patent made-up mixture available at shops that cater for the poultry-kepper. You can vary this with a wet or dry mash of blended poultry-meal. Greens are also necessary if your birds do not have access to grass and weeds in the garden. Don't forget that they also need clean drinking water.

Like other grain-eating birds, bantams need grit to grind the corn in their gizzards. You can buy grit mixtures for this purpose, made up of flint chippings and crushed shell to provide lime.

Health

Bantams, like other birds, are susceptible to parasites, particularly red mites. The birds themselves will deal with these, if given the opportunity, by taking regular dust baths. You can help them by providing a box of dry sand. Bantams will sift sand through every individual feather.

Breeding
There should be one cock to every 6 or 7 hens. Fence off the breeding nest with an enclosure of about 20 square feet.

Put dummy eggs in the nest at first, and when the broody hen starts sitting, replace these with eggs you want hatched. Keep the hen well supplied with food and water within the enclosure. The chicks should hatch in three weeks.

Peafowl

The full glory of a peacock's train is too well known to need description. But if these stately birds are going to grace your lawn there is a price to be paid. Peafowl are extremely strong and destructive, they tend to wander, and they have loud, raucous voices.

Buying
Peafowl are always expensive. They are not generally found in pet shops, but are often available from animal dealers who supply zoos.

Housing
If you are giving the peafowl the free range of your grounds and have any tall trees in the vicinity, they will happily find their own roosting places. Otherwise you will need an open-fronted shed or shelter of some sort, with high perches inside it.

Feeding

Peafowl are practically omnivorous. They will feed on insects, grubs, tender young shoots, and seeds. You can supplement this with a regular evening meal of poultry food. This will make the birds more confiding and less inclined to wander.

Health

Peafowl are generally healthy, hardy, and long-lived, but the chicks sometimes suffer from coccidiosis. This can be successfully prevented and treated by a patented preparation (available from your vet) that is slipped into the drinking water.

Breeding

If you provide suitable nesting sites, well covered and protected, within your garden, the hen will be likely to choose one of them, and is then less vulnerable to attacks from foxes, cats, and other predators. A clutch contains from 4 to 8 eggs, and these may be incubated by the peahen herself or by a broody domestic hen. Newly hatched chicks need looking after at first because the parents are liable to over estimate their strength and tax it to the utmost. Later the whole family presents a picture of harmony and solidarity.

It takes 3 years for the peacock to attain the full beauty of his plumage.

Pheasants

Among fancy pheasants can be found some of the most attractive and ornamental of all birds. Because they are essentially ground birds they make a pleasing contrast to the perching birds in an aviary, and they will not interfere with the other occupants.

Buying

Poultry trade papers will generally carry a few advertisements of fancy pheasants for sale. You merely have to choose the variety that most appeals to you and that you can afford.

Housing

An outdoor aviary is ideal for one or two birds, and they will grace any collection with their wonderful plumage.

Feeding

The food that drops from the feeding trays of the perching birds should provide your pheasant with the bulk of his diet. You can supplement this once a day with some greenstuff and small mixed grain.

Health

Pheasants are remarkably healthy birds and you should have few worries on that score. Most of the finest varieties are also quite hardy in Britain and need little or no shelter.

Breeding

For breeding purposes run a cock with 2 or 3 hens and put them in a separate enclosure, preferably with grass underfoot. There should be the odd perch or two in the enclosure as well as in the shelter that you must provide at one end of the run. This shelter can be open-ended but it must be roofed. Biscuit or dog meal, soaked in hot water or milk, is an important addition to the diet of breeding pheasants from late winter until early spring. Make sure that you collect all the eggs, because these can be laid almost anywhere. If for any reason you do not want the hen to incubate her own eggs, they can be artificially incubated or placed under a sitting bantam hen. Pheasant chicks should be fed little and often. Soaked biscuit meal, raw egg yolk, and finely chopped leaves are good.

A cock pheasant has to wait 2 years before his plumage attains its characteristic colour and sheen.

Kinds of pheasants

Two species that are often kept and are easily obtained are the Golden Pheasant and the Silver Pheasant. The *Golden Pheasant* is one of the smallest birds, and is also less expensive than most. The overriding impression is of golden yellow and scarlet plumage, with contrasting sheens of browns, greens, purples, and blues. The *Silver Pheasant* is a larger, heavier bird with a scarlet face. The upper parts and tail are silver, edged with black, while the crown and underparts are black and purple.

Quail

Quail belong to the poultry family, like pheasants and bantams, and are extremely ornamental as ground birds in an aviary of perching birds.

Buying
Quail are advertised for sale regularly in poultry magazines, and are not expensive to buy. You should get a true pair if you can, because cock and hen make a very devoted couple.

Housing
As ground birds in an aviary they soon get used to their new surroundings. They need a dust bath, and water for drinking purposes.

Feeding
Quail are omnivorous. In addition to seeds and grains of various kinds they will eat soaked biscuit meal and bread, insects, mealworms, and greenstuff.

Health
Quail are hardy, and after a period of acclimatization, will winter outdoors without coming to any harm. They are remarkably free from the usual bird complaints.

Breeding
A breeding pair should be given their own enclosure, with shrubs and clumps of grass or reeds in which to conceal the nest. The hen makes a scrape in the ground and lays

a clutch of several eggs (up to a dozen in some cases). She proceeds to incubate them for 20 days, with the male standing by all the time. He will also assist in rearing the chicks which, a few hours after hatching, are quite capable of running about and picking up food on their own.

Kinds of quail

Perhaps the most attractive species is the *Painted* or *Chinese Painted Quail*. It is the smallest of all the game birds—about the size of a day-old chick when fully grown. The cock has a black-and-white face and bluish grey chest and flanks. The bright chestnut on the under-parts contrasts with the yellow legs. The upper parts are mottled brown. The chicks of the Painted Quail are scarcely larger than bumble bees. This species makes a confiding pet, and can be given the freedom of a room.

Another beautiful and interesting species is the *Californian Quail*. The cock is altogether larger, with a black, forward-curving crest. It has a white forehead and a white band over each eye. The upper parts are mottled brown and the under-parts are blue-grey. There is a vivid pattern of white, black, and gold in the middle of the breast and belly. The hen is much duller. Although the Californian Quail is mainly a ground bird it will perch, especially at night, when it evidently feels safer off the ground. Pairs tend to quarrel among themselves, and can get quite aggressive towards their own offspring as they grow up. These quails also have a distinctive high-pitched cry.

FISH

Cold-water fish

Fish-keeping has been a popular hobby for thousands of years. Records show that the Chinese and the Romans enjoyed building aquariums and stocking them with exotic plants and fish. There is a lot to recommend fish as pets. While incapable, apparently, of marked affection for their owners, they have certain advantages over other popular pets. They are completely soundless, odourless, and inoffensive. They can be left for several days if necessary without harm coming to them. They are for the most part cheap and easy to buy, and cheap and easy to maintain and feed.

Fish use their fins, including their tails, to help them travel and change direction in water. They need oxygen in order to stay alive, but this oxygen, although it comes from the air, must first pass through the water to be of any use to them. Fish breathe through their gills, which filter the oxygen dissolved in the water, pass it on to the bloodstream, and expel carbon dioxide into the water. So when building and stocking your aquarium or pool, you must consider the surface area of water available for the fish to get their oxygen from, and to get rid of the waste carbon dioxide that they exhale. Artificial aeratous and oxygenating plants are useful aids in the provision of oxygen.

Fish can be divided into two main groups: those that will thrive in a cold-water tank or outside pond, and tropical fish that require heated water.

The Aquarium
Outdoors the ideal aquarium for cold-water fish is a pool in the garden. A newly constructed concrete pool must be given time to settle down before it is stocked with fish. Water frees poisonous substances from concrete that would prove fatal to fish. The safest procedure is to treat the water with potassium permanganate, leave it for a few days, then drain. After a thorough scrubbing, rinsing, and draining, refill with clean water and leave this to stand for a few more days before draining again. Refill with water again and let it stand for two or three weeks. Introduce the soil and selected water plants, and after a further fortnight or so you can begin to stock it with fish.

An indoor cold-water tank does not need quite the same precautions but it should be cleaned out thoroughly beforehand, and when the final water is poured in it should be allowed to stand for two weeks after the sand and plant life have been put in, before any fish are introduced. If the balance of water, plants, and fish is right a complete natural cycle of consumption and expulsion ensues, so that in theory you need never change the water. In practice you may have to do this two or three times a year with the best aquariums.

Water Plants

There are several plants that make oxygen and are therefore invaluable in the aquarium. Pondweeds, particularly *Canadian Pondweed,* are useful; so are *Vallisnaria, Ludwigia,* and *Myriophyllum.* These can be obtained cheaply from any aquarium stockist; he will also be able to recommend other suitable species. In an outdoor pool larger plants such as water-lilies can provide shelter and decoration.

Kinds of fish

The most popular and well-known of all cold-water pet fish is the *goldfish.* These fish are related to the carp and originally came from China. They have no teeth and so are inoffensive to other fish in the aquarium. Goldfish have been bred in a vast number of fancy varieties, and may be orange, white, black, red, or any combination of these colours. They are general feeders and will thrive on prepared fish food, breadcrumbs, earthworms, and small insects. Some varieties of the Common Goldfish are the *Veiltail*, the black *Moor*, the *Fringetail Goldfish*, and the *Lionhead*.

Other cold-water fish that make suitable companions for goldfish are the *Green Tench*, the lively *Minnow*, the *Golden Orfe*, and the *Golden Rudd*.

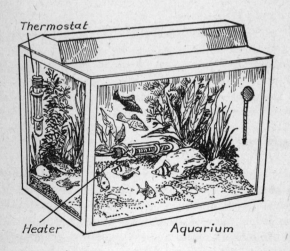

Thermostat

Heater   Aquarium

Tropical fish

Exotic tropical fish need warm water if they are to survive and multiply. The equipment needed to ensure their survival is not nearly as complicated and expensive as some people think. A rectangular plate glass tank with a metal framework forms the basic aquarium. It should have low feet, to lift it off the supporting surface, and preferably a glass top which can be raised about half an inch above the tank on rubber suction pads. This allows ventilation but stops the fish jumping out of the tank and outside objects falling in.

Electric heaters of various types can be bought. Some are immersed in a corner of the tank, others clip to the outside of it. They should be fitted with a thermostat, and the temperature set for about 70° F. Although fish require light, as well as warmth and air, they object to direct sunlight, so don't place your tank right in the sun's rays. For the bottom of the tank, use special sand that can be bought at any pet shop. This allows water plants to root and grow in it. You can landscape the bottom of the tank with decorative shells and rounded rocks and stones.

Siphon the water into the tank gently so as to disturb the sand as little as possible. When the tank is half full, insert the heater, and when all the water is in, switch on. The tricky business of pushing buoyant, flimsy, grass-like plants to the bottom and getting them firmly anchored there, takes practice. There are some implements, like miniature gardening tools, that will help you.

Suitable plants are *Cabomba, Echinodorus intermedius, Myriophyllum, Vallisneria,* and *Ambulia.* These can all be recommended, but your aquarium stockist will no doubt be able to show you his own list.

Kinds of fish

Tropical fish fall into two well-defined groups: those that give birth to living young, and those that lay eggs. A favourite among live bearers is the *Guppy.* It grows about 2 ½ inches long (female). The males are quite small and varied in colour. Guppies are lively, long-lived little fish, that need no artificial heat. Another live bearer is the *Platy*, which is available in a variety of colours. The *Swordtail* and the *Molly* are also popular live bearers, although they require a temperature of about 80° F.

Egg-layers include *Zebra* fish, tiny green-blue and silver fish; the inexpensive *Barbs* (*Cherry Barbs, Nigger Barbs, Checker Barbs*); the apparently luminous *Neon Tetras*; and the *Harlequin*, bright golden, with tiny black triangles superimposed.

Some tropical fish, such as the *Siamese Fighting Fish,* are extremely aggressive and cannot be put in the same tank with other fish. Make sure from your dealer that the fish you intend to buy from him can all live harmoniously together in one tank.

Feeding
Tropical fish should be fed, as much as possible, on live food. Daphnia, earthworms, Cyclops, and Tubiflex are all appreciated, but before you begin to wonder how on earth you are going to catch such strange-sounding creatures, it should be said that aquarists sell various packets of live food that are carefully balanced to provide everything your tropical fish need in the way of nutriment.

REPTILES

Tortoises and terrapins

Many people share an aversion to the very idea of reptiles as pets. They think of them as slithery, slimy creatures that bite or sting, or both. Nothing could be further from the fact. Many of the smaller reptiles make ideal pets for children. Tortoises, lizards and small snakes are smooth, dry, and pleasant to the touch. They are among the cleanest animals on earth, are quite inoffensive, and cheap to buy and maintain.

The Vivarium

A vivarium is a term used to describe the place where reptiles and amphibians are generally kept. Vivaria may be of the indoor or outdoor variety, and may differ considerably in size and nature according to the kind and number of animals you intend to house. Reptiles in general prefer to keep to dry land; some amphibians are partly terrestrial and partly aquatic, while others are almost entirely aquatic. So you have to cater for all tastes. Tropical specimens require a constant temperature of about 60° F. Outdoors your best plan is to enclose a portion of the garden with fairly steep, slippery sides of tiles or smooth stonework. Make it a yard high if you intend to keep frogs. The vivarium should have plenty of shade from direct sunlight.

Sink a pool in one end of the enclosure and see that it has some kind of steps to make it easy to get in and out of. If there are enough natural grasses and plants, and places to hide under and behind in the vivarium, your pets should be able to find most of their natural food without any extra feeding.

A fish tank, covered with sand along the bottom, makes a good indoor vivarium. Fill part of it with water and build up the remainder into a rocky and sandy bank. Plants, weeds, bits of bark, anything that will make a natural hiding place can be pressed into service. You really can't take too much trouble in landscaping the indoor vivarium. You can watch the inmates through the glass front. The top should be close-fitting with a number of ventilation

holes. Size will depend on the kinds of animals you are
going to keep, but generally speaking, the bigger the better.
Tropical creatures may need the use of a small heater
placed underneath the pool, but you may find that an
electric bulb, suitably darkened and placed above the roof
of the vivarium, will be adequate.

Tortoises

Tortoises are among the most popular pets for children.
Partly for this reason, and partly because of the enormous
traffic in these unfortunate animals due to popular
demand, few pets are so ill-treated and neglected. Very
little of this is deliberate—most of it is due to ignorance.
Many tortoises merely pine away because of inadequate
shelter or incorrect feeding.

The species usually offered for sale in pet shops is the
Iberian Tortoise, from southern Europe. It has a yellowish
shell with brown markings. The shell of a tortoise is
actually a prolongation of its backbone and ribs outside
the flesh. The underpart of the shell is a similar extension
of the breastbone.

Buying
Tortoises can be picked up for a few shillings in almost
any pet shop. Even though it is so cheap, it is worthwhile
examining your prospective purchase carefully beforehand. Choose one that is fairly heavy for its size; this
means that it has not been starved. The eyes should be

bright, and the hind legs should kick strongly when touched. The head should retract smartly within the shell when you try to touch it. See that there are no holes in the shell where a thoughtless dealer may previously have tethered the animal. Have a look round the outside and inside of the mouth to make sure that there is no fungus growing. When you get your tortoise home, place it in a shallow bath of tepid water. It will appreciate this and may also take a long drink.

Housing

The ideal place for a tortoise is a walled garden. Failing this there are several alternatives. A cool greenhouse, provided it is escape-proof, makes a good home. Or you can fence off a part of your garden with wire mesh and let your pet have the run of that. Make sure that there are no treasured vegetables or plants in the run, though, because he will make short work of those. His favourite is lettuce. Keep a pair of tortoises if you can. They are sociable and highly intelligent creatures, and solitary specimens will tend to roam in the spring. A pair will be more likely to make a true home of your garden, especially if they are fed with some titbit regularly at the same time and in the same place each day.

The sexes can easily be told apart by the shape of the breastplate. In the female it is flat, in the male concave.

If the tortoise has a run in the garden it will also require some sort of shelter at night and in wet weather (something a tortoise detests, incidentally). This can consist of a small box filled with leaves, or you can build a more elaborate den of wood or bricks with a sloping ramp to the entrance.

Feeding

Tortoises, contrary to a lot of popular opinion, are purely vegetarian in their diet, and it is no use your hoping that they will rid your garden of slugs and other pests. In the garden they will find their own food, which consists of lettuce, cabbage leaves, dandelions, chickweed, tomatoes, thistles, etc. But if for any reason they do not seem to be eating properly fresh greens can always be put out specially for them. In addition, of course, they must have drinking water in a shallow bowl. With a deep bowl they might either fall in or pull it over themselves in an effort to get a drink. They are also very fond of bathing, especially on hot summer days. A shallow tray full of water will be adequate for this. Shells can be groomed by polishing with olive oil.

Health

Although the list of diseases from which a tortoise *can* suffer is long and depressing, given the right conditions there is no reason to suppose that your pet will not stay healthy until the end of its days—which may add up to 25 years. Ticks are often present in the flesh. Soften the surface with vegetable oil, then the application of a little paraffin will loosen the tick's hold sufficiently for you to pull it out with tweezers. Canker is a yellowish, spongy growth round the mouth and on the tongue. This needs a vet's attention. In old age the shells start to flake and eventually pieces fall off. Long and brittle claws may have to be filed down, and running eyes need bathing with a solution provided by your vet.

Hibernation

In their native countries, tortoises hibernate at the approach of winter by burying themselves in the ground. If they try to do this in Britain they will find the ground too hard to get down deep enough, and they will not survive the winter. As soon as your tortoise looks as if it is preparing to hibernate (the signs are increasing sluggishness and a marked loss of appetite) prepare a box of dry earth and leaves. Put the animal in this and put the box in a cool spot in a shed or garage. If you wish to stop it hibernating at all you must keep it in warm quarters throughout the winter, both day *and* night. Any drastic fluctuation in temperature will kill it. Generally a tortoise that is allowed to hibernate properly will be all the better for it the following spring. Once it has settled down in hibernation, you must on no account disturb it. At the first signs of its awakening in the spring, provide it with water. It may not eat much at first, in spite of its weakened and emaciated state, but it will almost certainly be very thirsty.

Breeding

If you do have a true pair of tortoises, the female may eventually lay eggs. She does this very secretively in a hole about 5 inches deep that she scrapes with her forefeet. She buries the eggs so well that it is almost impossible to find them unless you have watched her in operation. They will never hatch in the cold ground, so if you are keen to have baby tortoises you must dig up the eggs and re-inter them, the same way up, in sand in a garden frame or hothouse. The temperature by day should be maintained around 80° F., and the eggs will hatch in about a month and a half.

Baby tortoises must be given the protection of an indoor vivarium at first, and fed on young lettuce leaves.

Kinds of tortoises

The two related species most frequently seen in the pet shops are Hermann's Tortoise and the Spur-Thighed Tortoise. *Hermann's Tortoise* comes from Mediterranean Europe, generally Italy. Both sexes have a claw on the tail and the segment of shell above the tail is double. The *Spur-Thighed Tortoise* has a kind of horny spur underneath each thigh. The upper jaw is slightly hooked, and the forelegs are twisted. The tail in the female is shorter and thicker than in the male. There is a single segment of shell above the tail. This tortoise comes from North Africa. The *Margined Tortoise* has an almost black shell with yellow triangular marks round the edges. It comes from Greece. *Horsfield's Tortoise,* from Asia, can be distinguished by its having only four claws on each foot, instead of the usual five.

Terrapins

Terrapins, or Water Tortoises, to give them their proper name, are delightful little creatures that will grace any vivarium. Although naturally about 8 or 9 inches long, they seldom grow larger than 3 or 4 inches in Britain. Their shells are very dark, relieved with irregular yellow splotches. They are much more active than land tortoises, are easily alarmed, and forage generally at night. Their hind feet are webbed for swimming.

Buying
Several species are often offered for sale in shops that specialize in creatures for the aquarium and vivarium. Prices vary according to species, but they are not costly creatures. When examining them for defects, be careful. Terrapins can give you a nasty nip with their sharp mouths.

Housing
A garden pond is the ideal home for these creatures, provided the surrounds are escape-proof. If you keep them in an aquarium you must also have somewhere, such as a raft or a bank, on which they can lie. Terrapins love to bake in the sun, and don't like to spend all their time in the water. Don't house them with small fish. Terrapins are carnivorous and will eat your small goldfish. The water must be cleaned three times a week, whether it is from an outdoor pond or indoor aquarium. Foul water will soon kill these animals.

Feeding

Terrapins will eat almost anything that moves in the water. They swallow their food under water, fighting for it, and following it with expertise. Small earthworms, meat scraps, grubs, insects, and small fish all come alike to the terrapin.

Health

Eye diseases and softening of the shell are the most common diseases that these reptiles suffer from in captivity. They are both attributable to foul water and lack of direct sunshine. Otherwise terrapins are remarkably long-lived creatures, some specimens attaining a century.

Hibernation

When winter approaches, those housed in an outdoor pool will try to bury themselves in the mud at the bottom and in this way may survive the cold weather. It is safer to bring them indoors to the warmth of an aquarium or vivarium.

Breeding

Terrapins do not breed in captivity, and very little is known of their breeding habits in the wild.

Kinds of terrapins

The *European Pond Tortoise* is a hardy terrapin, and is the one most usually offered for sale. It has a black body, dotted with yellow, and a long, pointed tail. *Reeve's*

Terrapin comes from Japan, and fully grown measures about 6 inches. It is the most striking of the hardy species, with a dark shell and yellow breastplate marked with black. It has a greyish-green head and neck.

The *Long-Necked Terrapin* is probably the most common non-hardy species offered for sale. It comes from Australia, and, as its name implies, its neck is almost as long as its body. The *Yellow-Bellied* or *Serrated Terrapin* comes from North America and is extremely decorative. Its dark brown shell is fringed with yellow. The underparts are entirely yellow, and there is some yellow between the eye and the mouth.

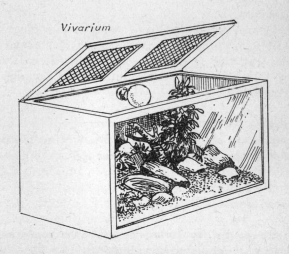

Vivarium

Lizards

There are more than 3,000 species of lizards in the world, varying widely in shape, size, and colour. A great many of them are better off in zoos than they are in private homes; these include the giant Komodo Dragons and the fierce iguanas of Central America. But most of the lizards available in pet shops are completely harmless, colourful, and delightful to keep. Lizards differ from snakes in having lids to their eyes and a solid jawbone. Snakes have a ligament at the chin which enables them to dislocate the lower jaw in order to swallow large prey.

Buying

There are so many different varieties for sale, costing anything from a few shillings to a few pounds that it would be impossible to advise on a good buy. When you pick up a specimen to examine it, shun the one that allows its head to droop. It will not last long in captivity. The correct way to pick up a lizard, by the way, is to grasp it firmly from above round the middle of its body with one hand, while supporting its weight from underneath with the other. If you take it by the tail, the tail is liable to come away wriggling in your hand. Although the animal will eventually grow another tail, it will be neither as long nor as colourful as the original.

Housing

All lizards love warmth and direct sunlight. British lizards can be placed in an outdoor vivarium, but imported varieties should be kept in an indoor vivarium at room temperature. If possible the enclosure should be easily portable so that it can be moved about from place to place in order to catch the maximum of sun. Electric bulbs, underfloor heating, and immersion heaters can supplement the warmth but they can never take the place of the real thing.

*   *   *

A flooring of fine peat, moss, and sand is ideal. There should be plenty of rocky retreats and places to sunbathe, growing plants, pieces of bark, etc. You must also see that there is water available for your lizards. Some species, like the chameleon, are almost entirely arboreal, and need branches along which to climb.

Feeding
Lizards live mainly on insects and similar small creatures: flies, spiders, caterpillars, gentles, and small mealworms.

Health
Lack of sunshine and inadequate ventilation are responsible for vitamin deficiencies, and these lead to sores and growths on the lizards' skin. Most lizards do not respond favourably to medical treatment.

Kinds of lizards

There are three species of lizards native to Britain: the Common Lizard, the Sand Lizard, and the Slow-Worm or Blind Worm. Of these only the *Slow-Worm* does well in captivity. It has been known to live for more than 30 years under good conditions. This legless lizard, often mistaken for a snake, can be found in almost any part of the country. It can also be bought very cheaply in pet shops. It grows to about a foot long, and is scaled all over. The upper parts are brown, the underparts black. It hibernates from autumn until late April. The young are born live in August and September. Slow-Worms feed largely on slugs, but they will accept spiders and earthworms. Although they appreciate warmth, they dislike direct sunshine and should have moist surroundings in the vivarium.

The *Common Lizard* does not live long in captivity, unless it is placed in an outdoor vivarium. It is a small lively creature, usually olive brown above and orange spotted with black below. A dark line runs down its back. The female is greyish underneath. It inhabits sandy heaths and commons, and produces three to six offspring, live and fully active. The *Sand Lizard,* again, does not take kindly to captivity. It is the largest and most colourful British lizard, but is rather difficult to find, being locally distributed. In its native haunts it is hardy and long-lived. It grows to about 8 inches in length, the male being dark brown above and paler below with dark spots. Its flanks are bright green with darker markings. The female is greyish brown above, with creamy white underparts.

The *Green Lizard* can almost be considered British—it is native to the Channel Islands. This species makes a magnificent pet, exceeding a foot in length. It becomes very tame in captivity, is no trouble to feed, and is highly intelligent. Its body is bright green, with yellow underparts. It is extremely fond of grasshoppers, and will breed in an outdoor vivarium. The *Wall Lizard* is a slim, attractive species from southern Europe. It gets its name from its habit of climbing up walls. It is extremely active and can run very fast. It is variable in colour, but in the breeding season the male is distinguished by green marks on its flanks. In addition to its usual insectivorous diet it also appreciates soft ripe fruit.

The *Glass Snake* is another legless lizard that resembles a large Slow-Worm. It comes from south-eastern Europe and grows more than a yard long. It has dark brown upper parts and reddish underparts, and its whole appearance is smooth and shiny, hence its name. It likes fairly moist, mossy surroundings, is easy to feed, and becomes extremely tame.

The *chameleon*, although essentially a lizard, has so many distinguishing characteristics, that it has been placed by scientists in a different sub-order, with about 50 different species. The chameleon is arboreal, and catches its prey by stealth rather than by speed of foot. It is incredibly deliberate in its movements and will lie motionless on a tree branch until some unsuspecting fly or other small insect alights within range. Then it suddenly unfurls its long curled up tongue with a movement too fast for the eye to follow, and transfers its prey to its mouth by means of a sticky pad on the end of its tongue. Chameleons vary from about three inches to more than a foot in length. Their bodies are covered in warty growths, and to add to their grotesque appearance their eyes can be revolved in opposite directions, independently. Each foot has five toes, two turning one way and three the other, giving the animal a secure grip on branches and twigs.

Although they like to lie in the sun, chameleons need a moist and humid atmosphere. They don't drink water but lick liquid drops hanging from the leaves. You will have to spray their enclosure once to twice each day to fulfil these conditions. Regrettably chameleons are notoriously short-lived in captivity, and unless you are very lucky will die after a few months. They are well-known for their colour-changing act. This does not vary so much with their background as with the prevailing temperature and humidity, and the animal's feelings at the time.

Snakes

Snakes are much maligned creatures. Many people think of them as cold, slimy, poisonous beasts that sting with their tongues. In fact many snakes make excellent pets. They are noiseless, inoffensive, clean, and long-lived. Their skins are not moist like those of amphibians, but dry. They are cold-blooded creatures, like lizards, and take their body temperature from their surroundings, so a snake in a heated vivarium will feel warm to the touch. Although there are more than 2,000 species of snakes only about an eighth of these are poisonous. All snakes have teeth, with which they bite. Poisonous snakes also have hollow or grooved fangs which are used solely for injecting poison. Their tongues, which often protrude and vibrate rapidly, are forked, and are used as organs of touch and smell.

Buying

Never buy a poisonous snake. The only venomous snake in Britain is the adder, and although it is not lethal to a healthy adult, the snake itself is invariably vicious and cannot be properly tamed. Most harmless snakes offered for sale are called "Grass Snakes". In fact, many of them are not Grass Snakes at all, but a similar species that is imported from Italy. Snakes vary in price from a few shillings to several pounds, the larger constrictors being priced at so much a foot. If in doubt about the good nature or otherwise of a prospective pet snake, watch the dealer handling it. If he takes extra precautions with it, such as using gloves, pass on to another pet even if he swears that the reptile is "harmless".

Housing

British and European species can be kept throughout the summer in an outdoor vivarium with a pond. Other species should be housed in an indoor vivarium, and the atmosphere kept warm and humid. The hotter it gets (within reason) the more active a snake is likely to be, and the readier it is to feed. So-called water snakes, which are almost amphibious in their habits, do well on an island surrounded by a shallow moat of water. A low outside wall with an inward overhang will effectively prevent their escaping. Dry land species need plenty of heather, sand, and peat, which retain some of the sun's heat.

*   *   *

Because snakes slough their skins several times a year, it is a good plan to provide water, in which they can soften their skins, and rocks and stones, which they can rub against to help the process of sloughing. In general it is wise to segregate the different species, because cannibalism is quite common.

Feeding
This is the one big snag with most snakes. In addition to being very erratic feeders (they will gorge non-stop for hours and then fast for weeks) they all prefer live food. In nature their diet consists of fish, birds, eggs, small mammals, other reptiles, mice, and almost any live animal that they can catch and kill. But in spite of opinion to the contrary, most snakes can be persuaded to take dead food.

Health
Snakes suffer from few diseases and will under normal conditions live for 10 or 20 years according to species. Occasionally they refuse all food and starve to death, and in such a case there is a way of forcibly feeding them before it is too late. It is really a job for two experts, and your vet should be able to advise you on this. Don't confuse this with a natural fast that may be taken after a heavy meal. When the snake is about to slough its skin it will also lose its appetite and become quite listless for a while.

Breeding

Most snakes lay eggs, but with some the young are born alive. Vipers and boas fall into the latter category. In the case of snakes that come from temperate countries, which retire into a state of semi-hibernation during the winter, mating usually takes place in the spring. Among well-known snakes that lay soft, shell-less eggs are the Grass Snake and the cobras.

Kinds of snakes

The *Grass Snake* is the largest and most common British snake. It grows about 3 or 4 feet long, and is greenish in colour with a yellow and black band just behind the head. In the wild these snakes put up a tremendous show of ferocity, hissing and striking, but they never bite. Anyone handling them at this stage is liable to have his hands covered with a foul-smelling liquid, which is the reptile's most potent means of defence. This, of course, does not happen when you handle a tame specimen. Grass Snakes are great swimmers, and they should always have an adequate supply of water available.

Another British species, although extremely rare, is the handsome *Smooth Snake*. It grows about 2 feet long and is steel grey in colour, with a row of black markings running the length of its back. It has a reputation for biting when first caught, but it quickly becomes tame. A beautiful imported species is the *Aesculapian Snake*, which comes from Europe and West Africa. It has a shiny brown body with very smooth scales. Unfortunately it does not take too happily to the vivarium, and bites rather freely. A less common species is the *Four-Lined Snake,* which is the largest European snake. It exceeds 6 feet in length and is yellowish brown with two parallel black lines running down each side of its body. It certainly is a most desirable snake—tame, intelligent, long-lived, will eat dead food and will not bite.

A popular imported species is the *Dice Snake.* It resembles the Grass Snake in appearance and in its habits, but is rather smaller. It is yellow, pale green, or grey, and its skin is marked with tiny black squares arranged in groups of five. It is a gentle reptile, never bites, is easy to feed (especially on fish), is long-lived, and tames quickly. Altogether it is highly recommended. The *Leopard Snake* is a hardy, long-lived, beautiful European snake, but it takes some acclimatizing to its new surroundings at first, and can be an awkward feeder. It is also a ready biter. It grows to a length of about 4 feet, brown above with reddish, black-edged spots, and rows of black, crescent-shaped marks down the sides. The underparts are chequered in black and cream.

Of the constrictors, *Boa Constrictors* are quite popular but rather expensive. They may grow to 12 or 13 feet in length, but provided you aquire a young specimen 2 or 3 feet long, you will have no trouble in taming it. This large heavily-built snake comes from South America, and makes an excellent pet. The more it is handled the more it seems to enjoy the experience. It is a handsome snake, light brown banded with darker streaks. The bars on its sides alternate with dark brown spots. A black band runs from its nose to its neck, and another one touches its eye. The underparts are cream with black spots. Its diet is mainly mice, rats, frogs, and birds which it squeezes and then swallows.

Pythons are the other large constricting snakes, some species of which make good pets. The most suitable is the *South African Python,* which is quite hardy, long-lived, and soon becomes extremely tame.

Tortoise

Grass Snake

Slow Worm

Sand Lizard

AMPHIBIANS

Frogs and toads

Amphibians are cold-blooded animals with backbones; they live part of the time on land and part of the time in water. Their skin is rather moist and smooth in most cases, and their body temperature varies with their surroundings. They lack the scales and claws of true reptiles. Most of them lay their eggs in water, and they are all carnivorous. Frogs and toads, newts, salamanders and axolotls are all amphibians. Some people dislike handling amphibians, but once they have got used to the idea they find that many specimens are charming, attractive, and a never-failing source of interest,

Frogs

Frogs are the least suitable creatures to keep in an indoor vivarium. They are generally quite active and their prodigious leaps will frequently end in their bruising and battering themselves against the side of the cage. The best place for them is outdoors. There they will thrive and may eventually learn to recognize you and approach for a regular feed.

Frogs are found almost all over the world. They live in wet and marshy regions, and are most active at dusk. They breathe through their lungs and partly through their skin, so if the skin is not kept moist the animals suffer. Out of about 1600 species of frogs in the world, only about a dozen are regularly kept as pets. A few frogs are almost permanently aquatic, but most are semi-aquatic. They lay their eggs in water, but come to the surface to breathe, and feed and hibernate on land. Many of them have loud voices that produce a monotonous one-note croak.

Buying

Frogs are not often offered for sale, but this is usually because of a lack of demand rather than a shortage of supply. Some of the more exotic species can be found in the larger stores, but even then they should not cost a fortune. Upkeep is low in the summer when there is an abundance of insects. Frogs are fairly easy to catch in the countryside at dusk, near ponds and streams, which are their natural homes.

Housing

Suitable vivaria have already been described, and of course the outdoor version is preferable for frogs. Many frogs are wonderful jumpers—their hind legs are specially adapted for the purpose—so make sure that the sides of the enclosure are fairly high, and that there is plenty of space for exercise. Do not try to keep outsize and tiny frogs together in one place. You will soon be left with big frogs only, after they have devoured their smaller brethren. Axolotls, tortoises, newts and lizards can be kept with the frogs.

Feeding

Frogs are carnivorous and will only eat a moving creature. If you are ingenious enough to make a piece of meat or a dead insect look alive you may induce your pet to swallow it. Generally frogs are not so easily fooled. This means that they must have a regular supply of live moths, worms, spiders, flies, and insects of all kinds. It is a further argument for keeping them outdoors where they can find a great deal of their food for themselves, as well as doing you a service by ridding the garden of many pests.

Health

Frogs are normally healthy creatures and fairly long-lived. Some frogs in zoos have lived for more than 20 years. If you do have an ailing specimen there is not much you can do about it apart from seeing that it is being properly housed and fed. Frogs dislike being handled too much—their skins are quite sensitive.

Breeding
The Common Frog lays large spherical masses of jelly-coated *spawn* (eggs) in stagnant water in February and March. When the tadpoles hatch they feed on water weed and other vegetable matter, but as soon as their hind legs appear they turn to a meat diet. After some weeks the tadpoles turn into tiny frogs and leave the water.

Kinds of Frogs

The *Common Frog* is well known and easy to find, but has nothing particularly to recommend it as a pet. It has a distressing habit of refusing to stay put, so unless your outdoor vivarium is virtually escape-proof you may have to replace these frogs with depressing regularity. The *Edible Frog*, on the other hand, will rarely stray from the sight and smell of its pool. This attractive animal is the largest of the European frogs. Its general colour is bright green, with a scattering of black spots and a yellow line running down its back. It may become finger-tame if you persist in feeding it at regular times. Even larger than the last species is the *Marsh Frog*. It is found in a number of places in Britain and lives well in a vivarium. Its back is greyish brown, and its underparts yellowish white. There are dark brown spots on its flanks and back, and bands of the same colour running across its hind legs. But like some other frogs, it changes colour to suit its surroundings.

An interesting and easily tamed species is the *American Bull Frog*, which is sometimes offered for sale. This animal exceeds 7 $\frac{1}{2}$ inches in length and can jump a tremendous distance. A large vivarium with a deep pool and a steady temperature of 65° F. are necessary for this species. Its body colour is olive brown with darker markings, while its underparts are yellowish white. Its notorious bellowing voice can be heard a mile away. In addition to the usual insects the Bull Frog will also eat other frogs and mice.

The *Tree Frog* is a delightful little grass-green creature. It is notable for its disc-like fingers and toes that are adhesive and allow it to climb up smooth vertical surfaces and cling to the underside of leaves. Tree frogs have smooth, soft upper parts, in various shades of green, and white underparts covered with tiny glands. These glands absorb water from the leaves to which the animals cling.

Because they spend most of their natural lives among trees, it is a good plan to instal them in a conservatory or greenhouse, if you can, always making sure that they have access to water. The European Tree Frog is the species most often offered for sale.

Toads

Toads differ from frogs in that their skin is dry, and generally rather knobbly and warty. Toads also differ from frogs in their habit of walking, rather than hopping. They are highly intelligent animals and make tame and interesting pets.

Buying
Like frogs, toads are not often seen in pet shops, and when they are it is usually one of the rarer species. The Common Toad can usually be picked up for a few shillings.

Housing
Toads can be kept in the vivarium along with some species of frogs, but ideally they should be given the liberty of the garden or greenhouse. Make a special home for your pet out of a large flower pot stood on its side, or a den built in the rockery, and he will take it over permanently. He must have water nearby, because he is semi-aquatic, although much more sluggish than a frog.

Feeding
Toads thrive on the same sort of diet as frogs, and are extremely useful in a garden because they will eat most of the pests. They are also extremely fond of earthworms.

Health
Toads are hardy and healthy, and have few natural enemies because their skin secretes an acrid substance when it is squeezed. Any predator with a toad in its mouth will drop its prey fast. They are notoriously long-lived creatures and may easily survive their owners. Toads also periodically cast their skin and eat it.

Breeding
The Common Toad will lay up to 7,000 eggs in two long strings, in stagnant water, in the spring. The strings of eggs are anchored to water weeds. The larvae appear

The *Natterjack Toad* is now rather rare, but still found in certain places in Britain. It is a small, agile animal with reddish warts on its back and barred hind legs. It has a yellow stripe all the way down its back, and its white underparts have dark markings on them. Its gait on land is a curious scrabbling lope, and it rarely goes near water except during the breeding season.

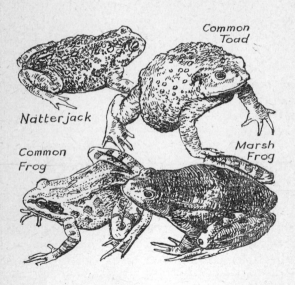

after about 10 days and feed on the jelly that h[
them. Later they hang on to the underside of the w
and begin to eat floating vegetable matter. It takes 85 (
for the eggs to turn into toads, when they leave the wa
A toad is not adult until it is five years old.

Kinds of Toads

In addition to the *Common Toad*, which is the easiest
acquire, there is a wide variety of species to choose fron
One sometimes offered for sale is the *Green Toad*, whic
comes from southern Europe. Overall it is light green wit]
dark splotches on its body. The *Midwife Toad* is a mos
interesting creature. The male takes charge of the incubation of the eggs. He wraps them round his hind legs in
long chains and carries them around for three weeks,
hiding in damp places. When the time comes for the
tadpoles to hatch, father toad takes to the water. This
toad is hardy and takes well to captivity.

The small *Fire Toad*, about two inches long, is mor
aquatic than most. It likes to float just below the surfac
of the water, with nostrils and eyes just visible. Its bac
is bluish black, very warty, but its belly is smooth, brigl
orange in colour, splashed with chocolate. These brilliaı
colours serve as a warning to its enemies that its sk
exudes a poison when punctured or roughly handled. Tl
Fire Toad is an agile diver and needs a fairly deep por
surrounded by peaty soil and damp moss. It hibernates
winter, but otherwise makes a charming and contented p

Newts, salamanders and axolotls

Newts are the only members of the Salamander family in Britain, and there are three species native to the country. They are almost entirely aquatic in the breeding season and do equally well in the pond of a vivarium or in a fresh-water aquarium. Domestic newts vary in size from about 3 to 6 inches in length. They are agile in water and can climb up the glass sides of a tank.

Buying
Many different kinds of newts are frequently offered for

sale in any pet shop that deals with water life, but the three domestic species can easily be found and caught in almost any pond or slow-moving stretch of water.

Housing

Whether your newts are housed in the vivarium or the aquarium, they must have access to water and land. In the aquarium cork rafts or islands or a sloping bank against the edge of the water will be necessary. The "land" must have a rock or two, or a similar cover under which the newts can hide.

Feeding

Newts are carnivorous, and will take their food on land or in the water. Any soft-bodied small creature will be eaten—worms, caterpillars, grubs, gentles, tadpoles, minced meat, even their own offspring.

Health

Fungus disease is always a possibility with newts. They get this through overcrowding, because they have a curious habit of cramming themselves all together in a favourite niche. See that there are not too many newts per square foot of space, and treat the fungus with paraffin. In spite of this hazard some newts have been known to live for nearly 30 years. Several times in a year newts cast their skins. These skins, when unbroken, are marvellous models of the ex-tenant, with every detail clearly etched, even to the toes on the feet. Newts hibernate either in the sand or in the mud at the bottom of a pool or they may sleep in a burrow on land.

Breeding

Most newts will breed in captivity. The breeding season starts in April, when the female lays a single egg, or batches of eggs, and attaches them to a water plant.

Hatching takes from 10 to 21 days, according to species and circumstances. The larvae have external gills, like tadpoles. These gradually become absorbed and eventually the larvae turn into complete newts. This process takes from three to five months, and then the young newts head for dry land. As soon as the young appear they should be removed to a separate breeding tank if they are not to become fodder for their unthinking parents.

Kinds of newts

The three newts found in Britain are the Common, the Crested, and the Palmate. The *Common Newt* is readily available in most ponds and ditches. It is between 3 and 4 inches long, and its colour is variable, usually greenish yellow or olive brown, with black spots. The toes are not webbed, and the skin is smooth all over. In the breeding season the male grows a low crest that runs down his back from head to tail. The *Crested Newt*, over 6 inches long, is the largest and most striking of the British species. Its back is olive brown with black spots. Underneath it is deep orange with black spots. Along its sides it displays tiny white dots. In the breeding season the male develops a high, saw-edged crest running the length of his back, and a silvery blue band appears on his tail.

The smallest of the British newts is the *Palmate Newt,* which grows up to about 3 inches in length. It differs from the Common Newt mainly in its tail which, instead of tapering gently to a point, ends in a short thread. Another major difference is that the male has webbed toes on his hind feet. This newt is olive brown in colour, with darker spots, some orange underneath, and a low dark crest in the breeding season.

The *Alpine Newt,* found in many parts of Europe, is a pretty species. It grows about 4 inches long, and is uniformly orange on its belly. The upper parts vary widely in colour, with dark mottlings. All varieties have yellow eyes and the usual breeding crest is also yellow, marked with black.

Salamanders

Salamanders are unmistakable creatures. They look rather like fat lizards, but they are true amphibians, without scales or claws. They are related to newts, but lack the conspicuous crest. In contrast to newts they are almost entirely terrestrial. They are slow-moving animals, spending most of the daylight hours hiding behind stones, rocks, or roots, and feeding at night. They have blunt heads, and their four-toed feet are not webbed. They vary in size from a Mexican species that is just over an inch long to the gigantic Japanese Salamander, which may attain a length of four feet.

The salamander's yellow and black markings are a vivid reminder to its enemies that its skin has a wealth of poison glands to protect it from being eaten. All kinds of legends have sprung up in the past about this meek and inoffensive creature. It was supposed to have supernatural powers for evil, to live in the fire and eat flames, and to be highly poisonous to all creatures, including man!

Buying
The *Spotted Salamander* is the species most often found in pet shops. It lives in many parts of Europe and is not expensive to acquire.

Housing
Salamanders may be kept in an outdoor rockery or in an outdoor vivarium, provided they have plenty of shade and shelter. They thrive best in an indoor vivarium, with plenty of moisture. They love cool, damp spots in which to hide during the day.

Feeding
Their favourite food is earthworms, but they will also accept snails, gentles, water beetles, slugs, grubs, flies, minced beef, and any slow-moving insects.

Health
Salamanders will live for a long time if properly looked after. There are records of some surviving for more than 70 years. The main dangers to their health are dry skin, and a fungoid growth caused apparently by overcrowding. Do not put too many specimens in one enclosure, and as

soon as you notice any fungus treat it with paraffin and rinse with clean water.

Breeding

Salamanders will breed fairly readily in captivity. When the female is ready to give birth she will lie half in and half out of the water. The 10 to 40 tadpoles that emerge are born live and will spend their first 6 months in water. At that stage they live on plant food and water fleas, and similar tiny animal life. When they come to land they are about 2 1/2 inches long, and begin to develop their well-known orange and black colour.

Kinds of salamanders

The *Common* or *Spotted Salamander* is about 6 to 8 inches long. It has a broad head and a stout body. Its general colour is black with vivid orange spots distributed all over the upper parts. The *Alpine Salamander* is a small slim species, black all over. Only two offspring are born at a time, fully developed from birth and equipped with air-breathing lungs.

Axolotls

Axolotls are curious, ugly creatures that look like enormous tadpoles. They are actually immature salamanders that can breed in their larval stage of development. Axolotls are sluggish, slow-moving creatures, fat, with a smooth, shiny skin blotched with yellow. They grow to about 8 inches long, with an enormous head, a tail encased in a broad fin, a dorsal fin, and four limbs. They have small brown eyes and a ruff on the nape of the neck formed of tufted, branched gills. They are nocturnal creatures and prefer to hide by day.

If you want to turn your axolotl into a salamander, gradually reduce the depth of water in its tank until there is not enough to cover it. This forces it to use its lungs. A covering of damp moss at this stage will ease its change into a complete salamander, a change that takes about a fortnight.

For a long time the axolotl was regarded as a separate species. Today it is recognized as the larval state of the Tiger Salamander that lives in Mexico and parts of the southern United States. In certain Mexican waters it remains an axolotl for the whole of its life, and although it breeds in this larval state, the offspring are invariably sterile.

Buying
Axolotls are widely imported for their curiosity value. Prices vary according to availability, the albino variety being the most expensive.

Housing
Axolotls may be kept in an aquarium or a vivarium equipped with a large tank. They are quite hardy and easy to keep. In spite of their sluggishness they are easily

frightened by a bang on the tank, and their general clumsiness tends to damage and break any but the stoutest water plants. Their tank should be kept out of direct sunlight, and they should have a rock or two to shelter behind. The water will need regular attention, with sediment being periodically siphoned off. Axolotls are best kept to themselves as they have a habit of attacking fish and newts in the same tank.

Feeding
They will eat almost any meat food, but if it is dead you must wave it about a bit to give it the illusion of life. Tadpoles, worms, fish, flies, earthworms, slugs, newts—all are acceptable to the axolotl.

Health
The axolotl is a most adaptable creature, and has no typical ailments. Specimens have survived, trouble-free, for 25 years in captivity.

Breeding
The best way to induce these animals to breed is to keep them for a while in a tank of water without plants. In summer transfer them to a larger tank with plenty of vegetation. The female will lay about a hundred eggs in bunches in winter or spring. These are attached to the water weeds. You must remove these eggs (or the parents) otherwise they will be eaten. The young hatch out in 10 to 20 days and should be fed at first on daphnia.

INSECTS

Silkworms and stick insects

Regrettably there are still many people today who are convinced that the only good insect is a dead insect, and even then they would rather not know about it. Many insects are beautiful to look at, and most of them are completely harmless. It cannot be said in all honesty that they show any great affection for their owners as pets, but the same can be said for most fishes, reptiles, and amphibians.

If you are keeping insects in the house, the first thing you will have to do is overcome this prejudice against your hobby by the other members of the family. The best way to do this is to keep the insects in your own room and make yourself entirely responsible for them. In this way you cannot be accused of sabotaging the bathroom or inducing hysterics in the kitchen. A second way out would be to have a small room (in the attic perhaps, or in the basement) specially set aside for your charges.

The main considerations are cleanliness, dryness, lack of disturbance, orderliness and, in the case of tropical insects, adequate warmth. Whichever way you go about it, you must be prepared to devote much time to your hobby.

Silkworms

The silkworm is the larva of the Common Silk Moth originally found in China some 4,000 years ago. Today it is commonly found all over the world, and is used extensively in the silk-spinning industry. Raising silkworms as a hobby provides a fascinating and inexpensive introduction to keeping insects in general.

The silk moth has a large, stout, whitish body, with comparatively short wings. Once the moths have freed themselves from their cocoons, they mate. The female lays upwards of 500 eggs and then dies.

Buying
The eggs are tiny, and cheap to buy. You will not need

more than about a hundred to start off with (in theory half an ounce will produce about 15,000 silkworms). Make sure, at the same time, that your dealer or some other source can offer you a regular supply of mulberry leaves. Otherwise you might as well forget about silkworms, because that is all they eat.

Housing and Feeding

If you buy your eggs in the autumn, and keep them at room temperature, there will be little change in them until the spring. Any increase in temperature will induce the eggs to hatch. Each day you will see them growing lighter in colour until eventually you will be able to hear the grub moving about inside the egg. After the worm has emerged, by biting a hole in the side of the egg, it will moult on the 6th, 10th, 15th, and 23rd days, gaining prodigiously in weight at each moult.

Feeding and housing are critical at this stage. Oblong wire trays are ideal receptacles for the worms. Each tray should hold about two or three dozen worms. Cover the worms with paper in which you have torn a few holes, and on top of the paper place the mulberry leaves. When they want to feed, the worms will crawl through the paper; this can be discarded and replaced with a fresh sheet each day.

The worms will not touch water, so make sure that leaves are completely dry before leaving them on the trays. They are also nibblers—that is, they prefer to eat round the edge of a leaf, especially in their young days. If you shred the leaves first, this will give the young worms a bigger biting area to work on. Keep the trays as clean as you can; any messiness will lead to disease. The worms will also be put off their food by sudden loud noises and changes in temperature or humidity.

Health

Unfortunately, losses among silkworms can be quite high on account of infectious diseases. A type of fungus quite often attacks them. The only practicable course of action in such a case is to cut your losses, get rid of the whole stock, and start again. Disease is encouraged by dirt and lack of proper ventilation.

Breeding

After the worm has finished its series of moults it will stop eating and its body will become transparent. This means that it is ready to start spinning itself into a cocoon.

Spinning usually starts about mid-summer. It will need an anchoring point for its cocoon. Anything fairly solid will serve for this—pieces of bark, the inside of a flower-pot, a small branch, or a bunch of heather. At this stage the temperature must be maintained at about 60° F., if possible, and the creatures left quite undisturbed. If you are going to breed from your moths, these will eventually emerge from the cocoons. If you want to try your hand at silk-spinning, dip the complete cocoon in acetic acid.

While keeping silkworms is an unusual hobby for a pet keeper, it is difficult, indeed, and can be time consuming.

Stick insects

Stick insects look exactly like twigs. Their camouflage is so perfect that they are almost impossible to see when surrounded by natural twigs and branches. Unlike most insects, they do not have wings. They come from the Middle East and belong to the same family as grasshoppers and crickets. The thin body is about 6 inches long, and the legs are long and awkward-looking, slightly knobbly to resemble a bent twig. Stick insects are green or brown in colour, with darker varieties also available. They moult several times during their lives, and when frightened they pretend to be dead.

Buying
Stick insects are readily obtainable at many pet shops and are usually cheap to acquire. Their upkeep is low provided you have access to a privet hedge.

Housing
Stick insects are not fond of strong light. A well ventilated box is ideal if kept at normal room temperature. Several stick insects may be kept together, although if they do not get enough of the right kind of food they tend to start eating each other. But don't keep other insects with them—they look too much like tasty twigs.

Feeding
The usual diet is privet leaves, although ivy leaves may be accepted as a substitute. They tend to absorb moisture through their food and, except when newly hatched, or

about to die (wen they can no longer eat), they won't touch water. Leaves should be left on the stem, and the whole stem standing in a jar of water. But make sure that the insect cannot fall into the water. Change the food every other day. The insects will only refuse it if ailing or during a moult. After each moult they will need a lot more food than before.

Health

Fungus, that bane of insect life, is again the chief trouble. It arises from overcrowding, bad ventilation, and lack of cleanliness. If your insects are obviously badly affected it is best to put them out of their misery and start again with fresh stock. But first thoroughly clean out and disinfect the box. Under ideal circumstances, stick insects will live for about 15 months.

Breeding

Stick insects can reproduce themselves without the aid of a male. Thus deprived of a job, the male is a very rare customer indeed. He is a much thinner insect, with longer legs. Egg-laying does not start until the mother is about 9 months old. About 500 eggs are usually laid, and these are scattered about all over the box and completely neglected. If you want them to hatch you must gather them up and put them into a suitable container at room temperature. Then you have a long wait—it may be as long as 10 months; but the average time for hatching is nearer 5 months.